Classic Catfish
from
The Crown at The Antique Mall

Evelyn and Tony Roughton

Illustrations by
Kevin O. Roughton

Published by THE ANTIQUE MALL, LTD.
P.O. Box 540
Indianola, Mississippi 38751
1-800-833-7731
Printed in the U.S.A.

Illustrations by Kevin O. Roughton
Edited by Martha N. Weeks
Calligraphy by Vicki T. Pentecost
Design Consultant Jennifer Roughton

First Printing   5,000 books   March, 1993
Second Printing   7,500 books   September, 1993

ISBN 0-9635571-0-6

Printed in the USA by

WIMMER

The Wimmer Companies, Inc.
Memphis • Dallas

Especially for Charles —
How long for you to
come again..!
See you again
at home !
Evelyn

Dedication

This book is dedicated to Jennifer and Kevin,
who have given us so much help and love.

Best Fishes !
Evelyn Royliton

Acknowledgements

There are so many people we have to thank for helping us over the years that we have had THE CROWN AT THE ANTIQUE MALL! Mac and Snooks McDade, Evelyn's parents and our partners when we first opened the shop in 1972, have helped in too many ways to even think of naming. They have always given us their love and support, even when they thought we were crazy. We've had a good time in this family venture! And we love and thank them for the chance to try it!

Jennifer and Kevin, our talented children, have been an integral part of the growth of our business and this cookbook, from concept to actual design. Kevin's illustrations are truly outstanding! His design for the cover and format of the book, combines an idea by Keith Daniels, photography by Leigh Sanders and calligraphy by Vicki Pentecost. Kevin and Jennifer's help, advice, and confidence in us has made this the ultimate family project.

Martha Weeks, has given us months of editing, typing, tasting, cooking, suggesting, implementing, helping in every way with the book and with our shop. We are so grateful for a friend like Martha! Without her, this would still be a "good idea," and not reality.

Mary Lee McKinney, who has worked with us almost as long as we've had THE CROWN, has tested endless recipes, developed great ideas and taken so much responsibility from Evelyn's shoulders! We thank her for that special help!

Denise Smith, Kathy Myrick, Ann Hendon, Janice Butler, who work with us at the shop and take good care of it when we are gone — we thank you for your suggestions, your help and loyalty.

The entire catfish industry has supported our efforts to create a Gourmet Catfish and we thank them for their help. We deeply appreciate the leaders in the industry bringing their clients, visitors and the news media to THE CROWN AT THE ANTIQUE MALL for lunch and to just browse around and taste our SMOKED CATFISH PÂTÉ. And we want to thank the catfish farmers who helped us experiment with everything from fingerlings for frying to roe for caviar.

From the beginning of our mail order PÂTÉ business, we have gotten orders and encouragement from the Catfish Farmers of America, the processing plants, The Catfish Institute, The Catfish

Women of America, Mississippi State's Food and Fiber Center, the aquaculture scientists for Mississippi State, Auburn University and Stoneville, so many individual catfish farmers and families, banks and businesses in the Delta and from Mississippians who said they were proud to share our PÂTÉ with their friends across the country. We thank you all!

Our special thanks to our friends and family! Edward Britt, Evelyn's uncle, who helped us build the special smoker for our fish! Ren Hinote's special input and ideas! All those who shared their recipes with us, gave us ideas, encouraged us, tried our recipes and ate pounds of catfish with us while we were writing this book!

And our grateful thanks to God who gave us these friends and family and all of our many, many blessings!

Evelyn and Tony Roughton

Introduction

THE CROWN

Our little restaurant opened in 1976 in the back of our English antique shop. To create the ambience of an English pub or village tearoom, we named it THE CROWN and furnished it with antique tables, chairs and accessories from the shop. We still maintain that same look sixteen years later.

Opening a Georgian antique shop in the middle of a cotton field, fully five miles from the nearest town, required plenty of extra effort and optimism. We knew we had to do something very special to entice people to come. The reward for our efforts was overwhelming support from the townspeople from the very beginning. In the early days my sister, Wanda, Mother and I did all the cooking and serving. Wanda's bread is still the crowning glory of every meal, and Mama's Caramel Pie has not been equaled since she retired. (She can still be prevailed upon to pitch in on busy days.)

We have loved sharing the lives of the many friends we've made in the shop and restaurant. THE CROWN has been the setting for birthday parties, wedding rehearsal dinners, bridesmaids' luncheons, debutante brunches, and hundreds of bridge parties. We have entertained clients from Japan, Spain, Germany, Thailand, Russia and Belgium for the catfish and cotton industries. We've served them apple pie, iced tea and catfish every way but fried!

We've shared numerous pots of tea with very special friends, and staged coffees, christening parties, class reunions, graduation fetes, formal teas, fashion shows, art exhibits, groomsmen's brunches, and family dinners with five generations present. We've hosted a wedding reception, little girl tea parties, businessmen's lunches, wedding and baby showers, cocktail buffets, and my parents' Fiftieth Wedding Anniversary party. There have been many cozy afternoons when close friends gathered to celebrate a birthday, a college homecoming, or a trip to Europe. Meals have been shared with families and friends from as close as Jackson, Mississippi, and as far away as London, England. Many times busy young mothers have spent just a few relaxing moments around the Dessert Cart before picking up children from school.

THE CROWN has been hard work at times, but we have received so much pleasure from it. Our customers have become friends we will treasure forever: in that simple fact lies the pure joy of this business. Thank you all for making our little restaurant, way out in the country, work so well for so many years!

Evelyn Roughton

Coming of Age

In the Mississippi Delta, when someone invites you over, and says "We're going to cook fish," you can rest assured you've been invited to a FISH FRY! There will be coleslaw, hushpuppies, french fries and plenty of it!

Family fish frys were a real treat when I was young. My Uncle C.E. would get a really hot fire going under an enormous black iron kettle, way out in the back yard, sometimes at his house and sometimes at my grandparent's house on Shackleford Lake. All the men would stand around in the shade watching the fish and then the hushpuppies cook, sizzling away in the bubbling hot grease. It was an all day affair, of course, the result of a fishing trip to Six Mile Lake or Mossy Lake! The fish back then *was* river catfish—and it still tasted wonderful! Muddy flavor and all!

All that has changed now. We still have fish frys, and the men still stand around outside watching the cornmeal on the fish sizzle, but the kettle is now a specially made, gas fired cooker, the grease is peanut oil and the fish come from the processing plant, already cleaned, skinned and filleted!

Farm-raised catfish are a delight to cook! There is always a consistent, sweet flavor. None of the oily, fishy smell and taste that is present in so many other varieties of salt water and fresh water fish. Quality, safety and consistency of flavor make farm-raised catfish the joy of health conscious consumers.

Farm-raised catfish are a phenomenon! Twenty years ago there were a few catfish ponds scattered around the Mississippi Delta. There were a few people experimenting with the novel idea of fish farming and there were some ponds put in strictly for pleasure fishing. Now there are nearly 120,000 acres of commercial catfish ponds and it has become the largest farm crop in our area. Bigger even than cotton!

Visitors to the area wonder at the miles of water they see on the side of the road. A lot of them know about our catfish industry and come here especially to see it, but others think the ponds are rice fields or just can't believe that all that land is dedicated to growing catfish! We see a lot of tourists at THE CROWN AT THE ANTIQUE MALL, and we love to tell visitors all about the farms, the processing, and naturally, we insist they try our SMOKED CATFISH PÂTÉ even if they aren't staying for lunch—which always includes a catfish entree!

Years ago, when the industry was smaller, we could call the great folks at our local processing plants, tell them we had customers at the shop from Wisconsin or California or wherever and someone would drop what they were doing and take our visitors on a tour of the plant. They were shown the quality control laboratory where fish from each pond are cooked and tasted numerous times before that pond is harvested and brought into the plant for processing.

They could see the water-filled trucks full of fresh, live fish seined just hours earlier from ponds only a few miles away. They could watch as those live fish were funnelled from the truck into holding tanks and into the plant. Within 30 minutes of leaving the holding tank, those live fish become quick frozen fish fillets! Now that is fresh fish!

The processing plants have grown so much now that individuals can no longer tour the plants. Now we just try to explain in words and pictures how this industry produces fish that are safe, free from pollution and chemicals, nutritionally outstanding and fresher than most people can believe is possible. We can still arrange visits to many of the catfish farms in the area, however. These generous farmers have shown visitors the hatcheries, arranged for them to see the feeding and harvesting, and even gotten on buses with tour groups from all over the country, to explain the unique levee systems, aeration techniques and 24 hours a day work involved in producing this unusual farm product.

At the shop and at the numerous food shows we attend each year to sell our SMOKED CATFISH, we explain to our customers that catfish is no longer the legendary bottom feeding, river catfish they might have fished for in their childhood. These "pedigreed" farm-raised catfish are bred to come to the top of the pond to be fed, just like goldfish in your aquarium at home. The feed they receive is made especially for them with nutrients and natural grains. The water they swim in is monitored day and night for the correct temperature and oxygen content to produce a mild, sweet tasting fish without the oily, fishy smell and flavor of so many ocean fish.

Cooking with catfish is a joy because there are no fishy flavors to overcome! The sweet meat of the catfish will absorb any flavor you choose to give it. A soft butter sauce, a classic Hollandaise, the smokey goodness of the grill—your choices are unlimited. What we've done in this cookbook is give you specific instructions for a huge variety of dishes. But we have also given guidelines for your own experiments in cooking. Try any of your own recipes but substitute farm-raised catfish for the meat—recipes traditionally made only with salmon, or chicken, or even beef. Try our Southern Catfish Sausage and you will understand just how adaptable this fish really is!

Catfish can be purchased in stores nationwide now and through the efforts of the Catfish Farmers of America, The Catfish Institute and the Catfish Associations in the many states that now produce farm-raised catfish, consumers are being made aware of the quality, ready availability, nutritional value and exceptional versatility of this once maligned creature of the rivers. Now the thoroughbred of the fish industry—FARM-RAISED CATFISH!

Useful Information & Techniques

Poaching

Many of the recipes in this book refer to poaching the fillet, or chunks of the fillet! One of the greatest things about catfish is it's ability to take on the flavor of the ingredients in which it is immersed. So poaching the chunks of fish in a rich tomato and basil sauce will give the sauce the advantage of the fish juices being blended with the sauce to make it even richer, and it will preserve the pieces of fish intact in the shape you have cut them! Cooking fish chunks in crab boil or Old Bay Seasoning will give you a crab-like consistency and flavor. *Et cetera, et cetera, et cetera.*

The key to poaching, is to bring the liquid only to the barest simmer and hold it there while the fish is cooking. Put the fish in the simmering liquid, bring it back to a slight shiver and cook it only 8 to 10 minutes. You have to judge the time according to the depth of the liquid and the thickness of your fillets. When the fish is nicely white all over and firm to the touch your fish should be poached properly. If you have chunked the fish, the time will be shorter, of course. The number of dishes created by poaching catfish is limited only by the imagination of the cook!

The liquid left by the poaching is full of flavor and should be incorporated into the dish if at all possible. Reduce the amount of liquid by bringing it to a full boil and cook until the volume is reduced by one-half or two-thirds. Whisk butter into the liquid and the resulting sauce is delicious! Or simply freeze the reduced liquid to use at another time.

Frying

We have given several specific recipes for frying catfish. Again this is a time that you can be creative. Spices in the coating you use can vary tremendously! You can rub the meat of the fish with a pre-pared mustard before coating. Or soak the fillet in a Tabasco sauce mixture. Some people swear by white cornmeal and others prefer yellow meal. Becky and Jimmy Walker at CICEROS soak their catfish in a beer bath before coating it with cream-style cornmeal. And their fried catfish is outstanding!

Cornmeal coatings are traditional throughout the South, but you can also use the standard seasoned flour-beaten egg—flour dipping method of coating foods to fry. Be creative!

A number of these recipes call for BUTTERMILK! If you don't have it on hand, a good substitute is 1 cup of milk and 1 tablespoon of lemon juice or vinegar. Mix and let it sit at room temperature for about 15 minutes. Or use 1 cup of plain yogurt to equal to 1 cup of buttermilk. These substitutions are not as good as the real thing— but they will work!

Peanut oil does seem to be the frying oil of choice! It heats faster to a higher temperature, so the food cooks quicker, absorbing less of the oil.

Grilling

Fish, especially the fillet, cooks very quickly on the grill, so watch it carefully! Be sure to preheat the grill, oil the cooking surface of the grill, and use an oily-buttery basting liquid or marinade for the fish in most cases. Use a bed of vegetables or lemon slices, under the fillets as they cook on the grill to give the fish flavor and protect it from the direct heat of the fire.

Baking and Broiling

These techniques are standard of course, but just remember **DO NOT OVERCOOK!** Fish cooks quickly! Overcooking means that the texture will be ruined, the juices evaporated and the flavors lost! There are recipes that call for long baking times, but usually the desired result in those cases is a crisp outside coating while retaining a moist interior.

We like to use individual serving dishes to capture all of the juices that escape in the cooking process. Those captured juices even in large baking pans, can be poured over the finished dish, enhanced by a squeeze of lemon or a bit of butter!

Nutrition Information: *per 1 ounce of raw catfish fillet*

Calories	Protein	Fat	Cholesterol	Carbohydrates	Sodium
46 cal.	5.57 gm.	2.64 gm.	23.23 mg.	0.00 gm.	0.08

Table of Contents

"And you thought it had to be fried"

Appetizers

Avocado and Catfish Dip

4 catfish fillets
2 cups chicken bouillon
1 cup fresh lime juice
1/3 cup thinly sliced celery
1/3 cup minced red onion
2 tablespoons chopped green pepper
1 tablespoon chopped parsley
1 cup chili sauce
2 teaspoons bottled horseradish
1 avocado, cut in 1/2 inch pieces

Wash the catfish fillets. Cut the fish into 1-inch pieces. In a saucepan, bring the bouillon and catfish to a boil. Cut the heat off and let the fish cool in the broth.

In a glass bowl, mix the lime juice, celery, onion, green pepper, parsley, chili sauce and horseradish. Add the cooled and drained catfish pieces, tossing gently to mix with the sauce. Do this at least 24 hours ahead, if possible, so that the flavors will blend nicely. Just before serving, remove from the refrigerator and gently add the pieces of avocado. Pile into a pretty glass bowl and serve with pita bites or melba toast.

Serves 12

The colors of this dish are beautiful on a buffet table—and so are the flavors! Joy Tindall Aden gave me this recipe a number of years ago to prepare for her father, Frank Tindall's birthday party. I've used it many times and love it!

Try serving it as a salad as well. Drain it a bit, pile it on pretty lettuce, with extra slices of avocado and tomato surrounding the catfish chunks. With warm pita bread or hot rolls, it makes a great first course or luncheon dish.

Catfish Beignets

1 cup water
6 tablespoons butter, in pieces
1 teaspoon salt
1/4 teaspoon cayenne pepper
Tiny pinch of nutmeg
1 cup all-purpose flour
4 eggs
2 to 3 catfish fillets (1 cup ground)
1-1/2 tablespoons chives
1 tablespoon mixed Italian Seasonings
Peanut oil for frying

Bring the water, butter, salt, pepper and nutmeg to a boil in a large, heavy saucepan. Boil slowly until the butter has melted. Remove from the heat and immediately add all the flour stirring vigorously until the mixture is blended. Put the pan back on the heat, and cook for a few minutes, beating continuously until the mixture pulls away from the sides of the pan and forms a smooth mass. Remove from heat and beat in the eggs one at a time, being sure that each one is fully incorporated in the mixture before adding the next egg. Set the pastry mixture aside.

Wash the catfish fillets and pat very dry. Cut in 1-to 2-inch chunks and put into a food processor. Process the raw fish until it is finely ground. You will need 1 cup of ground fish. Pat any excess moisture from the ground fish.

Add the ground fish, chives and Italian Seasonings to the pastry mixture, beating long enough to mix thoroughly.

Heat the oil to a good frying temperature. Drop the beignets into the hot oil using a rounded 1/2 teaspoonful as a measure. They will be fairly small and will cook quickly. Cook until nicely browned and serve immediately. (They are even good cold!)

Makes about 50 bite-size Beignets

This is basically a recipe for a cream puff paste with the addition of the catfish and seasonings. Experiment with your own variation of seasonings! Try the hot beignets dusted with Parmesan cheese. Or add a tablespoon or two of whipped cream to any leftover mix, spread it on bread rounds and bake in a hot, 400° oven for 12 to 15 minutes until puffed and browned.

Capered Catfish Chunks

8 catfish fillets
3 cups water
1/2 onion, thinly sliced
Juice of 1 fresh lemon
1/2 teaspoon pepper
1/2 teaspoon salt
2 bay leaves

Marinade

1 cup olive oil
3/4 cup vinegar
1/4 cup sugar
2 teaspoons salt
1 teaspoon dry mustard
3 bay leaves
2 cloves garlic, minced
2 teaspoons chopped parsley
1/4 cup capers

Wash the catfish fillets and cut into 1-inch, bite-sized pieces. Poach gently in water flavored with the onion, lemon, pepper, salt and bay leaves. Cook in 2 or 3 batches, to prevent crowding the fish. Lift the fish from the water and set aside.

Mix all 9 ingredients for the marinade in a large bowl. Gently add the cooked catfish pieces, turning to coat well. Cover and refrigerate for at least 4 hours or overnight.

Serves 12

This party dish can be made 2 days in advance. Serve the catfish bites in a pretty glass bowl with wooden picks on a buffet table. Or do individual servings by piling the catfish bites on plates lined with sliced cucumbers. Serve with toasted pita triangles.

Chili Catfish Cocktail

4 catfish fillets
3 teaspoons Old Bay Seasoning
4 cups water
2/3 cup chili sauce
1/2 cup ketchup
2 tablespoons horseradish
Juice of 1 lemon
Grated rind of 1 lemon
1 teaspoon Worcestershire sauce
4 drops Tabasco
Salt to taste
Shredded lettuce

Wash the catfish fillets and cut in 1-inch pieces. Place pieces in a saucepan with 4 cups of water and the Old Bay Seasoning. Bring to a boil, then cut off the heat and let the catfish cool in the seasoned water. Refrigerate until needed. This step may be done as much as 2 days ahead. The flavor will just improve with time.

Carefully mix all the remaining ingredients, except the lettuce, in a small glass bowl. Cover and refrigerate until needed. This sauce will hold for 3 to 4 days.

When ready to serve, shred lettuce very finely. Place it in a stemmed glass and pile the cold, seasoned catfish pieces on top. Cover the top of the catfish with the cocktail sauce and serve immediately.

Serves 4 to 6

Instead of the traditional stemmed sherbet or champagne glass for the presentation of this appetizer, try using cleaned scallop shells, avocado halves with just a bit of shredded lettuce to decorate the cavity and the rest underneath the avocado shell, or giant lemon halves, emptied of the pulp and juice and layered with the shredded lettuce, catfish and sauce. Gorgeous and delicious!

Citrus And Catfish Saté

4 catfish fillets
Juice and zest of 1 lemon
2 tablespoons olive oil
1/2 teaspoon ground cumin
2 tablespoons white vinegar
1/4 teaspoon cayenne pepper

Wash the catfish fillets and pat dry. Cut the fillets into long, thin strips. Mix the remaining ingredients in a small bowl. Add the catfish strips to the bowl and stir to coat the strips with the marinade. Continue to stir occasionally while the fish marinates—up to 2 days.

When ready to serve, skewer the catfish strips on metal or wooden picks. Grill over a hot fire for 2 to 3 minutes on each side. Serve immediately with a squeeze of fresh lemon or with a Lemon Sauce.

Serves 8 to 12

For a cocktail buffet service, the Indonesian Catfish Saté and the Citrus Catfish Saté look great piled on a platter together. The Citrus Saté is light in color and the Indonesian Saté is dark with the soy marinade, but the same sauces compliment both styles. I like to cover a platter or tray with magnolia leaves, use a glass bowl in the center of the tray for the sauce, circle the bowl with the skewers, piling them up to the level of the bowl, and garnish with a bright lemon "flower" and another magnolia leaf.

Creole Catfish Cakes

1 pound catfish fillets, broiled
6 tablespoons butter
3/4 cup flour
2 cups milk
1/2 teaspoon salt
1/2 teaspoon black pepper
1/2 teaspoon dry mustard
1-1/2 cups finely chopped bell pepper
1/2 cup finely chopped green onions
1/2 teaspoon Tabasco
1-1/2 cups fresh bread crumbs

Melt the butter in a heavy saucepan. Add the flour. Stir constantly for 2 to 3 minutes, while the roux bubbles. Add the milk slowly, continuing to stir until the cream sauce is thick, 10 to 12 minutes. Add salt, pepper and mustard, mixing well.

Flake the catfish fillets into a bowl. Add the cream sauce and the remaining ingredients, mixing thoroughly. Use the fish mixture immediately or refrigerate for up to 2 days.

Using a large spoon, make cakes with the fish mixture and coat them completely with more fresh bread crumbs. Using a heavy skillet, sauté the patties gently in 1 tablespoon oil and 1 tablespoon butter, until they are browned. Keep warm while you continue cooking the cakes, adding more oil and butter as needed.

Serves 8 or more

This recipe is perfect for using your imagination! The cakes can be made large enough for a luncheon serving or tiny to serve as pick-up appetizers. They are delicious served with a fruit salsa. Or use them as a base for poached eggs with a Hollandaise Sauce over the top. Fill mushroom caps with the fish mixture and bake for a great hot appetizer. Or fill green peppers with the mixture and bake for a wonderful hot main dish.

Crunchy Fried Catfish Bites

4 catfish fillets
3-ounce package Ramen noodles
4 tablespoons flour
1/8 teaspoon salt
1/8 teaspoon pepper
3 large egg whites
Peanut or vegetable oil for frying

Cut the catfish fillets into bite-size pieces. Wash and pat dry. Place the noodles in a plastic bag and crush into tiny pieces. Mix the flour, salt and pepper in another bag. In a bowl beat the egg whites until foamy.

Place the catfish pieces, a few at a time, into the flour bag and shake to coat. One at a time, coat the pieces with the egg white and the noodles. Let the pieces sit for a few minutes while you continue to coat the others.

Fry the catfish pieces, a few at a time, in the hot oil until they are golden, 1 to 2 minutes. Serve immediately.

Serves 8 to 10

Serve this quick snack with a sweet and sour sauce for dipping or a pretty Plum Sauce. Crunchy Fried Catfish could easily be a main dish allowing 1 fillet per person. Serve over rice and drizzle the good sauce over the fish.

Plum Sauce

1-1/2 cups red plum jam
1-1/2 tablespoons prepared mustard
1-1/2 tablespoons prepared horseradish
1-1/2 teaspoons fresh lemon juice

Mix all ingredients in a small saucepan. Heat until the jam is melted and the sauce is blended. Serve immediately or cool to room temperature. Store refrigerated.

Makes 1-1/2 cups

SMOKED CATFISH
Custards

2 fillets of SMOKED CATFISH
(available at specialty food stores or by mail order see–index)
4 eggs
1/2 cup whipping cream
2 cups milk
1/4 teaspoon cayenne pepper
1 cup grated Cheddar cheese
2 tablespoons butter, softened

Flake the SMOKED CATFISH and set aside. In a small bowl, lightly whisk together the eggs, cream, milk and pepper. Butter generously 8 large custard cups or ramekins. Divide the flaked fish between the custard cups, topping the fish with the cheese. Fill the cups with the egg mixture. Set the cups in a pan that will hold 1/2 inch of water and the cups. They will cook more smoothly and evenly in the water bath, but they can go straight onto the oven racks.

Bake in a preheated 350° oven for approximately 30 to 35 minutes. They should be puffed, firm and browned. Remove from the oven and serve immediately.

Serves 8

Custards are a classic English starter and the lovely flavor of the SMOKED CATFISH is subtle and delightful in this creamy dish. Try the custards for lunch or supper as the main dish, with fresh steamed vegetables and an avocado and orange salad. Colorful and delicious!

Delta Catfish Croquettes

1-1/2 pounds catfish fillets
6 green onions, minced
1 egg
2 tablespoons grated fresh ginger
Juice of 1 lemon
1/2 teaspoon salt
1 teaspoon pepper
Vegetable oil

Using a food processor, coarsely chop the catfish fillets. In a glass bowl, mix the fish with the remaining ingredients, blending thoroughly. The mixture can be refrigerated at this point for up to 24 hours.

When you are ready to cook the croquettes, heat 1 tablespoon of oil in a heavy non-stick skillet. Using a teaspoon, form small rounds and sauté the croquettes until they are browned on both sides, 2 to 3 minutes. Add more oil as necessary until all are cooked. Drain on paper towels and keep warm.

Makes 25 to 30 croquettes

These bite-size croquettes are wonderful finger food. Garnish them with a tiny slice of peeled lemon and a touch of parsley. They are even good served cold with a Cucumber Sauce. The mixture makes a great stuffing for small mushrooms—stuff and bake at 350° for about 15 minutes. Serve hot. They are super!

Cucumber Sauce

1 small cucumber, grated
1 clove garlic, minced
1 cup plain yogurt
1 teaspoon fresh lemon juice
1 tablespoon chopped fresh mint leaves
1 tablespoon minced green onions

Mix all ingredients well. Add salt only if you need it. Refrigerate for up to 3 days. The sauce tastes fabulous served with our SMOKED CATFISH FILLETS. Try it!

Makes 2 cups

Goat Cheese and Catfish Canapes

1 catfish fillet
4 ounces mild goat cheese
2 tablespoons minced sun-dried tomatoes
2 tablespoons minced parsley
1 tablespoon minced green onion
1 dash Tabasco sauce
18 to 20 freshly cut bread rounds

Poach the catfish fillet gently for about 8 minutes. Set aside to drain and cool.

Flake the catfish into a small bowl. Add cheese, sun-dried tomatoes, parsley, green onion and Tabasco. Stir vigorously until thoroughly mixed.

Spread the catfish mixture onto the bread rounds, dividing it equally. Place bread rounds on a cookie sheet. This can be done one hour in advance. Refrigerate until needed.

When ready to serve, broil for 1 to 2 minutes under a pre-heated broiler. The rounds will be slightly puffed and lightly browned. Serve immediately.

Makes 18 to 20 canapes

Use these bite-size treats as a passed Hors d'Oeuvre for a formal meal or use them to round out a light meal of soup or salad. That's when the leftovers come in! You can even use leftover fried catfish—just knock off the breading and flake. This is such an easy recipe and it looks like "time and trouble."

Indonesian Catfish Saté

16 wooden skewers
1/4 cup soy sauce
1 tablespoon vinegar
1 teaspoon packed brown sugar
1/4 teaspoon ground ginger
1 clove garlic, crushed
4 catfish fillets

Soak the wooden skewers in water and refrigerate for 1 hour. This will help to prevent the wood from burning during cooking.

Combine the soy sauce, vinegar, sugar, ginger and garlic in a small bowl. Stir well to dissolve the sugar. Set aside.

Cut the catfish fillets, lengthwise into four thin strips. Two of the strips will be longer than the others. Thread 1 catfish strip onto each wooden skewer. Cover the catfish skewers with the marinade and refrigerate for several hours.

When ready to serve, grill the skewers for 3 minutes per side and serve warm on a bed of Cucumber Salad as a first course or from a buffet table with a choice of sauces.

Makes 16 small skewers

Cucumber Salad

2 cucumbers, thinly sliced
1 onion, thinly sliced
1/2 cup vinegar
1/4 cup water
1/2 teaspoon salt
1 teaspoon liquid non-sugar sweetener
1 tablespoon chopped parsley

Place the cucumbers and onions in a glass bowl. Add the remaining ingredients and mix thoroughly. Refrigerate for several hours if possible.

This salad will hold refrigerated for several days.

Serves 4 to 6

Jalapeño Catfish Rolls

3 cups cooked catfish, poached
  or broiled
3/4 cup chopped green onions
6 tablespoons chopped, pickled
  jalapeño peppers
1-1/2 cups grated Monterey Jack cheese
1/2 cup prepared tomato salsa
1 package phyllo pastry
1/2 cup melted butter

Chop the cooked catfish and place in a bowl. Mix the catfish, onions, peppers, cheese and salsa. Taste and adjust the seasonings if you like an extremely hot flavor. This is hot, but not unbearably so. Set the catfish mixture aside.

Melt the butter and set aside. Open the box of phyllo pastry and unroll the sheets. Keep the sheets covered at all times with waxed paper and a slightly damp cloth, and work as quickly as you can. On a flat surface, lay out one of the sheets of phyllo. Brush it generously with butter, and place a second sheet of pastry directly on top. Brush it with butter also, and continue with the third and fourth sheets of phyllo.

On the long side of the pastry, using 1/3 of the catfish mixture, spread the filling along the long side of the pastry within 2 inches of the long edge and 1 inch of the short sides. Rub butter on all sides of the pastry. Fold the short sides over the ends of the filling, enclosing the edges. Fold the long side over the filling and roll up the pastry. Seal the top edges of the pastry with the butter. Place seam side down on a lightly greased baking sheet. Rub the top and sides lightly with butter. Continue with the rest of the filling and more pastry.

Bake in a preheated 400° oven for about 20 minutes, or until nicely browned. The rolls can be served immediately or refrigerated until needed and warmed to serve.

Makes 3 rolls of 12 slices (36 bites)

I like to make this ahead of time, cut the rolls when they are

well chilled and serve them at room temperature.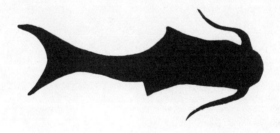
They can be a bit messy to eat with your fingers,
but sliced and piled on a pretty platter with a dish
of extra salsa, the rolls are a great party food. Make
the rolls smaller by cutting the phyllo in thirds before
rolling and serve them as a main dish. On a plate of finely shredded lettuce with tomato salsa, guacamole and beans—a super
meal!

Phyllo pastry is scary for some people, but it so much fun
when you start to use it. It tears easily, but a little butter and
another sheet will "patch" any holes you make. An extra sheet to
repair a tear or a hole will only embellish the final dish—so
there's no need to worry about mistakes. You can enclose almost
anything in phyllo and it will taste great! Filled pastries freeze
well so you can do them ahead, cooked or uncooked. Read the
instructions on your box well and just forge ahead with the phyllo.
You will have extra sheets when you finish this dish, so you can
either wrap the sheets carefully and use them later, or experiment
with everything in your refrigerator and wrap it all in phyllo!
Just have fun with the pastry!

Mississippi Party Mold

2 cups cold poached catfish
1/2 cup cold water
1 teaspoon paprika
2 envelopes unflavored gelatin
8 ounces cream cheese
1/3 cup mayonnaise
1/2 cup minced celery
1 tablespoon chopped parsley
1 tablespoon grated onion
1 tablespoon lemon juice
1 teaspoon Worcestershire sauce
3 dashes Tabasco
1/2 teaspoon salt, or to taste

Flake the catfish and set aside. Mix the paprika into the 1/2 cup of water and let it sit for a few minutes. Add the gelatin to the water, letting it soften and then dissolve the gelatin over low heat.

In the large bowl of an electric mixer, beat the cream cheese and mayonnaise until smooth. Add the dissolved gelatin, the catfish and the remaining ingredients. Mix until well blended. Pour the mixture into a decorative mold and chill.

Serves 25

I always use a fish mold for this delicious spread. The paprika gives the mixture a pale pinkish color and a touch of flavor. If you prefer a whiter mold, do not use the paprika—the taste is still wonderful.

You might try this in individual fish molds as a main dish for a salad luncheon! It's rich but delicious. Serve it on a bed of sliced cucumbers and slivered raw carrots with tiny hot rolls and fresh fruit.

Oysters And Catfish Chervil

1 pint oysters
4 catfish fillets
1/2 cup butter
1 teaspoon chervil
1 teaspoon Fine Herbs

Drain the oysters in a colander. Wash the catfish fillets and pat dry. Cut the fillets into 1 inch pieces. Set aside.

Melt the butter in a chafing dish or skillet. Add the Herbs and stir to blend. Add the oysters and the catfish pieces, stirring to coat with the butter mixture. Cook for 2 to 3 minutes over low heat, stirring occasionally. It is ready to serve immediately from the chafing dish. Heap toast points around the base of the chafing dish and let the party begin!

Serves 20

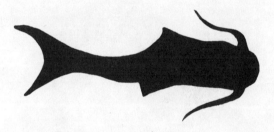

On a cocktail buffet table, this is fabulous! The textures of the oysters and catfish are a good contrast, and the juices blend wonderfully. And it is easy! It can be last minute or you can actually cook it before the guests arrive and warm it to serve. Just do not overcook!

Mary Sferruzza gave me this recipe using oysters when we were planning a party together! Adding the catfish just makes it more of a Delta party dish! Mary and Bobby always made their parties come alive with energy and originality. We all miss Bobby!

Presbyterian Day School SMOKED CATFISH Log

2 SMOKED CATFISH FILLETS
(available at specialty food stores or by mail order—see index)
8 ounces cream cheese
1 tablespoon fresh lemon juice
1 teaspoon prepared horseradish
2 teaspoons grated onion
1/4 teaspoon salt
2 tablespoons chopped parsley
1/2 cup chopped pecans

Flake the SMOKED CATFISH FILLETS into a mixing bowl. Add the remaining ingredients and mix well. Chill for several hours. Mix the parsley and pecans. Shape the chilled fish mixture into a log shape and roll in the nut mixture. Refrigerate until needed.

Serves 20

Several years ago, Vicki Harrell and the Presbyterian Day School in Jackson, Mississippi, used our SMOKED CATFISH FILETS to create this super recipe for a fund-raising event. We loved it! And you, too, will love this simple and delicious recipe!

Rockefeller Catfish Tarts

10-ounce package frozen chopped
   spinach
2 green onions, chopped
2 anchovies, chopped or 1 teaspoon
   anchovy paste
3 dashes Tabasco
2 garlic cloves, minced
1 teaspoon Worcestershire sauce
2 tablespoons lemon juice
1/4 cup sour cream
2 tablespoons butter, softened
Anisette, to taste (optional)
3 catfish fillets
Grated Parmesan cheese
Pastry rounds

Thaw the spinach and drain well in a colander. Place in a
kitchen towel and squeeze out as much liquid as possible.

Combine spinach, onions, anchovies, Tabasco, garlic,
Worcestershire, lemon juice, sour cream, butter and anisette in
a blender or food processor. Mix thoroughly. Set aside.

Cut catfish fillets into 1-inch pieces. Wash and pat dry. Set
aside on absorbent paper.

Cut rounds of pastry to fit small muffin pans or tart pans.
(Short pastry or puff pastry will work.) Press pastry rounds
into the pans. Place 1 piece of catfish in each tart shell. Cover
each tart completely with the spinach mixture. Top each tart
with a sprinkling of Parmesan cheese.

You may prepare the recipe ahead to this point and refrigerate for several hours. When ready to serve, bake in a preheated 375° oven for 15 to 20 minutes to cook the pastry and
lightly brown the cheese.

Makes 24 tarts

*An elegant appetizer with very little work! You could use
cleaned oyster or clam shells instead of the pastry shells for a lovely plate presentation. These pastries are wonderful passed or on a
buffet table—they aren't a bit messy and pick up easily.*

Puff Pastry Fish Stuffed
With SMOKED CATFISH PÂTÉ

1 pound SMOKED CATFISH PÂTÉ
(available at specialty food stores or by mail order—see index)
2 SMOKED CATFISH FILLETS
(available at specialty food stores or by mail order—see index)
2 sheets puff pastry
1 egg, beaten, for glazing and sealing

On one of the sheets of puff pastry, draw an outline of the fish you want to serve. (Of course, my fish has large whiskers and a curve in his tail because he is always a CATFISH!) When you are happy with the outline, using a sharp knife, cut the puff pastry in a fish shape. Lift the fish and place him onto the second piece of puff pastry. Draw around the fish, but make this fish about 1 inch larger than the original. Cut out the second fish with a sharp knife.

Place the smaller fish on a baking sheet covered with aluminum foil. Cover the fish with the SMOKED CATFISH PÂTÉ leaving a 1/2 - inch strip along the sides. Carefully pile the minced SMOKED CATFISH FILLETS on top of the PÂTÉ spreading evenly. There should be a nice mounded effect. I like to use a lot of the PÂTÉ and SMOKED FISH. Gently rub the uncovered edge of pastry with the beaten egg. Place the larger fish on top of the smaller. Pat the fish gently before you seal the edges to remove any air pockets. Seal the edges together with a fork or by pressing with your fingers and gently rolling the cut edges. I like to press and roll the edges so the fish shape is sharper.

You can decorate the top of the fish with the bits of leftover puff pastry. Use a sharp knife and give him an eye, more whiskers, lines in his tail—be creative! Use the beaten egg to "glue" each pastry piece to the body of the fish. When you have finished decorating, rub the entire fish with the beaten egg and bake. Follow the cooking directions for the puff pastry that you are using, but a general guide is to place in a 425° oven for about 30 minutes, until puffed and golden.

When the fish has cooled, carefully place him on the

serving dish of your choice, lifting the foil and
pulling it back gently, to allow the fish to
"peel off" directly onto the serving piece.
Refrigerate until served.

Serves 20

*This really is a spectacular party dish and it is so easy to do!
The fish can be made in any size you choose—the directions are
the same whether you are making a fish to serve 50 nestled on a
silver platter on the buffet—or one fish for each guest as a show
stopping first course! The pastry fish should be made and baked
just a few hours before serving for the best results. Slicing is
neater and the pieces are easier to handle. If you cannot find puff
pastry at your local market, packaged crescent rolls will work.
The pastry is not as interesting, but the technique is the same.*

Rollmops
(Marinated Catfish Rolls)

> 1-1/2 cups white vinegar
> 2 white onions, thinly sliced
> 1 teaspoon mustard seeds
> 2 bay leaves
> 1/2 teaspoon ground allspice
> 3 whole cloves, crushed
> 1/2 teaspoon coarse ground black pepper
> 1/4 teaspoon sugar
> 4 catfish fillets
> 1/2 cup Dijon mustard
> 1/4 cup small capers, drained
> 1/2 cup chopped white onion

Place the first 8 ingredients in a heavy pan and bring to a boil for 2 to 3 minutes. Set the marinade aside. Let it cool slightly while you cut and roll the catfish.

Wash the catfish fillets and cut in half down the center. Spread the mustard, capers and chopped onion along the length of the 8 pieces of fish. Carefully roll up each piece, securing with wooden picks. Stand the rolls on end in a deep dish that will hold them in one layer.

Pour the warm marinade over the rolls and refrigerate, covered, for at least 4 days so that the Rollmops will "pickle" properly. Drain the marinade to serve.

Serves 20 (Serves 4 as a main dish)

For a cocktail buffet, use 1 or 2 rolls for a garnish on the platter. Unroll the others and cut them into bite-size pieces. They can be placed on rounds of buttered brown bread or just piled on the platter and served with wooden picks.

The Catfish Rolls will hold nicely for 10 to 12 days. They also make a great supper dish served with hot boiled potatoes, salad and brown bread.

This is a traditional European dish made with herring—and if you are a Rollmop fan, you won't believe how delicious Catfish Rollmops taste!

Seviche

1-1/2 pounds catfish fillets
3/4 cup fresh lime juice
2 cups chopped fresh tomatoes
6 green onions, finely chopped
2 tablespoons chopped fresh parsley
1 teaspoon dried oregano
1/2 teaspoon hot chili powder
3 tablespoons white vinegar
1/4 cup olive oil

Slice the catfish fillets down the center to make 2 long pieces. Then cut at an angle into 1/4-inch thick pieces.

Pour the lime juice into a glass or ceramic bowl. Add the catfish pieces, mixing well. Cover and refrigerate for 4 to 5 hours, stirring occasionally as the fish marinates.

In another bowl, combine the remaining ingredients, mixing well. At the end of 4 hours, carefully add the fish and lime mixture to the tomato mixture, stirring gently but thoroughly. Chill the Seviche for at least 4 hours or up to 24 hours before serving. Drain off the liquids as you serve.

Serves 20 (Serves 4 as a main dish)

Serve this traditional Spanish dish as an appetizer with brown bread and butter triangles or as a light meal with a mixed green salad. Catfish is a very untraditional fish to use for Seviche, but perfectly demonstrates its versatility!

Spinach and Cheese Bites

**4 cooked catfish fillets, poached
  or broiled
10-ounce package frozen chopped spinach
2 tablespoons butter
1 teaspoon garlic powder
1 medium onion, chopped
8 ounces Feta cheese, crumbled
3 ounces cream cheese, softened
1 egg
1 teaspoon nutmeg
Salt and pepper to taste
1 package phyllo pastry
1/2 cup melted butter, or more**

Flake the cooked catfish fillets and set aside. Thaw the spinach and squeeze it in a cloth until as much moisture as possible has been removed. In a medium skillet, melt the butter and cook the onion and garlic for 1 to 2 minutes. Add the spinach and toss in the hot skillet to release the rest of the moisture. Be careful not to brown.

Transfer the spinach mixture to a bowl and add the cheeses, egg and seasonings. Mix thoroughly. Add the flaked catfish and blend well. Taste the mixture and adjust the seasonings. The filling may be made ahead to this point and refrigerated for up to 24 hours.

When you are ready to roll the pastries, melt the butter and unroll the package of phyllo. Place 1 sheet of phyllo on your working surface, keeping the others covered with waxed paper and a slightly damp cloth. Brush the phyllo sheet with the butter and cover it with another sheet. Continue with a third and fourth sheet of phyllo. Divide and cut the stacked sheets into 4 long strips. Brush the edges of each strip with a little butter, place a rounded tablespoon of the filling at the end of each strip. Fold the end of the strip over the filling, forming a triangle. Continue folding up the strip, enclosing the filling with each fold, and rub the last bit of phyllo with butter to seal the triangular package. Rub the surface of the package with butter and put on a baking sheet.

Continue making the triangles of pastry until all the filling is used. The Catfish Bites may be made ahead to this point and refrigerated until ready to bake. Bake in a hot oven, 400° for about 12 to 15 minutes, or until browned. Serve hot.

Makes 16 to 20 Catfish Bites

For a cocktail party, you cannot ask for an easier dish to make ahead and still serve it hot and wonderful from the oven. The Catfish Bites can even be frozen and baked right out of the freezer. You can make them smaller by cutting your phyllo in five or six long strips instead of four. Just adjust the amount of filling.

This can be a great main dish as well. Make the spinach and cheese mixture without the cooked catfish. Position a whole uncooked fillet on the sheets of phyllo cut in half lengthwise, and top with the filling. Roll and seal the phyllo with butter and bake about 20 minutes. Really good!

Torta of SMOKED CATFISH

2 SMOKED CATFISH FILLETS
(available in specialty food stores or by mail order— see index)
16 ounces cream cheese
Juice of 2 lemons
2 teaspoons Tabasco
4 green onions, chopped
1 tablespoon capers, drained
1 hard boiled egg, minced

Chop the SMOKED CATFISH FILLETS and set aside. In an electric mixer, place the cream cheese, lemon juice and Tabasco. Mix until the cream cheese is fluffy and soft.

On a footed cake plate, make a round of the cream cheese mixture at least 1 to 2 inches inside the edge of the plate. Smooth and flatten the first layer of the Torta. Sprinkle 1/2 of the chopped SMOKED CATFISH over the cream cheese. Add a sprinkling of green onions, approximately half, on top of the chopped fish. Put the second layer of cream cheese on top, smoothing carefully. Cover with the rest of the green onions and SMOKED CATFISH. Scatter the drained capers evenly over the Torta. Cover carefully and refrigerate until needed. Try to assemble a few hours before using so that the flavors have a chance to blend. Just before serving, sprinkle the minced egg over the top and garnish the Torta with lemon slices and mint leaves.

Serves 25

The blend of flavors is wonderful in the Torta! The smoke is very subtle and the textures are nice. I like to serve it with a very plain water cracker, or toasted pita triangles. The pedestal presentation allows you to generously pile the crackers on a tray beneath the cake plate, which should eliminate any refilling during the party.

Soups

Cajun Catfish Soup

3 catfish fillets, diced
2 tablespoons olive oil
3 green onions, chopped
1 clove garlic, minced
3/4 cup dry red wine
3 level tablespoons ketchup
1-1/2 cups chicken broth
1/4 teaspoon black pepper
1/2 teaspoon oregano
2 tablespoons chopped parsley

Heat the oil in a heavy saucepan. Add the green onions and garlic. Cook 1 minute. Add the diced fish and continue to cook until the fish is white, stirring constantly. Add the remaining ingredients to the pan. Stir gently to combine well. Simmer for 20 minutes.

Serves 4 to 6

Serve the soup immediately or refrigerate for 1 to 2 days before using. I like to toast a piece of buttered French bread and serve the soup poured over it in a bowl. The color of the fish is a little strange because of the red wine, but just relax, the flavor is rich and lusty and the color mellows as the soup simmers.

Catfish Chowder

4 catfish fillets
2 cups water
4 cups diced potatoes
4 cups diced onions
1 cup milk
1 cup cream
1/2 cup butter
1/4 teaspoon thyme
1 teaspoon salt
1/2 teaspoon pepper, or to taste

Cover the catfish fillets with water and simmer until fish flakes, about 15 minutes. Remove the fish and set aside. Add potatoes, onions, thyme, salt and pepper to the broth and simmer until vegetables are cooked, about 30 minutes. Add the milk, cream, butter and fish. Mix well and correct seasonings, if necessary. The chowder can be refrigerated at this point for 1 to 2 days. Heat and serve.

Serves 4 to 6

Soups are fun to make in great quantities—especially in the winter. Catfish chowder freezes so well you can happily plan on leftovers without feelings of guilt or worry about waste.

Delta Bisque

2 large catfish fillets
1 tablespoon butter
3 green onions, chopped
2 stalks celery, finely chopped
1/3 cup butter
1/3 cup flour
4 cups milk
1 cup cream
1 teaspoon Tabasco
1 tablespoon chopped parsley
1 bay leaf
1 tablespoon chopped chives
1 teaspoon salt, or to taste

Wash the catfish fillets and cut into 1/2-inch pieces. Place in a large heavy boiler with 1 tablespoon butter, onions and celery. Simmer slowly for 3 or 4 minutes, but do not brown. Remove fish and vegetables. In the same pan, melt 1/3 cup butter. Add the flour and stir 2 to 3 minutes to cook the flour. Slowly add the milk and cream, continuing to stir while the bisque thickens. Add the catfish mixture and the remaining ingredients. Simmer very slowly for 15 minutes. Serve immediately or the Bisque may be refrigerated for up to 3 days.

Serves 6 to 8

This lovely thick bisque is excellent served with pasta. A bowl of your favorite pasta, covered with "leftover" soup makes a meal that is easy and delicious!

Great Gumbo!
(Catfish, Of Course!)

1/2 cup vegetable oil
1/2 cup flour
4 garlic cloves, minced
2 cups chopped onions
1 cup chopped celery
1 cup chopped green bell pepper
10 ounces frozen cut okra (optional)
16-ounce can chopped tomatoes, with
    liquid
5 cups chicken stock
1/2 teaspoon cayenne pepper
1 teaspoon salt
2 bay leaves
1 pound sliced smoked sausage,
    Andouille or other
6 catfish fillets, washed and chopped

Make a roux with the oil and flour, browning it slowly and stirring frequently. Cook over medium heat for about 30 minutes until it is a rich, milk chocolate color. When the roux is just right, add the garlic, onions, celery and green pepper, stirring vigorously. Cook 2 to 3 minutes. Turn the heat to low and cook 15 to 20 minutes, stirring occasionally.

Add the remaining ingredients and simmer for one hour or more. Don't completely forget about the gumbo on the stove, but it doesn't need a lot of attention at this point. Stir it just because it smells so good and you can't keep your tasting spoon out of it!

Taste for seasonings and add pepper or salt as you choose. You can also add a variety of seafood to the gumbo—shrimp, crab meat, crawfish—whatever is on hand! Wonderful to keep in the freezer for unexpected company or a quick supper when you need a "pick-me-up."

Makes 3 quarts

Mississippi Catfish
Court-Bouillon

3 pounds catfish fillets
1/2 cup vegetable oil
1/2 cup flour
1 cup minced green bell pepper
1 cup minced celery
1 cup minced onion
16-ounce can Hunt's Special Sauce
4 cups tomato sauce
1 gallon water
1 cup minced green onions
2 tablespoons Worcestershire sauce
2 teaspoons salt
1-1/2 teaspoons red pepper
1-1/2 teaspoons black pepper
1 teaspoon garlic powder
3 teaspoons paprika
2 bay leaves

Cook the catfish fillets by poaching or broiling. Set aside.

In a very large, heavy saucepan, heat the oil and add the flour, stirring constantly to make a roux. Allow the flour to become a rich, nutty brown, the color of milk chocolate, but DO NOT BURN the roux.

Add all the ingredients, except the catfish, and combine thoroughly. Let the mixture simmer for 30 minutes.

Add the cooked catfish and simmer for another 30 minutes, stirring frequently. Adjust the pepper to suit your personal taste. You may want it hotter than we like it—so if you feel like a true Cajun, pour in more pepper or Tabasco!

Serve immediately or allow the flavors to blend in the refrigerator for up to 2 or 3 days before serving. Serve in a bowl over rice as a first course soup, or in larger servings as a filling main dish with hot French bread on the side.

Makes 1 gallon—plus some
Serves 8 to 10

I know this recipe makes an enormous amount, but for very little effort you can eat well tonight and fill the freezer with portions of soup for later. Or share it with your friends, the way our neighbor, Bethel Martin, did when she brought us a quart of this wonderful broth and told us to enjoy it! She brought the recipe back from a Louisiana trip, made a few changes, and even convinced herself that she likes catfish another way than fried!

Red Bean And Catfish Chili

2 tablespoons vegetable oil
1 large onion, minced
3 garlic cloves, minced
2 tablespoons chili powder
1 teaspoon ground cumin
1/2 teaspoon ground coriander
1 teaspoon cinnamon
1 teaspoon oregano
1/2 teaspoon cayenne pepper
16-ounce can tomatoes, with liquid
1 large green bell pepper, diced
16-ounce can kidney beans, drained
  and rinsed
1/2 teaspoon salt
Pepper to taste
1 pound catfish fillets, diced

In a large saucepan over medium heat, cook the oil with the next 8 ingredients for 2 to 3 minutes, stirring constantly. Add the tomatoes, green pepper, kidney beans, salt and pepper. Stir for one minute. Place the diced catfish fillets on top of the chili mixture and gently stir them into the chili. Turn down heat and simmer for 15 minutes. Serve immediately.

Serves 2 to 3

It's a real bonus when great tasting food is easy to prepare and is also healthy. When you make this chili, you have the best of all worlds. The recipe doubles easily and will hold until the next day if you need it to. It will even freeze. Serve this with a good Mexican corn bread and a green salad. Delicious!

Southern Catfish Stew

1 pound catfish fillets
3 slices of bacon, chopped
1 cup chopped onion
1/2 cup chopped green pepper
1 large can tomatoes
2 cups peeled and diced potatoes
1 cup water
1/4 cup ketchup
2 tablespoons Worcestershire sauce
1 teaspoon salt
1/2 teaspoon pepper
1/2 teaspoon thyme

Wash the catfish fillets and cut into 1-inch pieces. Set aside. Fry the bacon for 2 to 3 minutes in a large heavy saucepan. Add the onion and green pepper. Cook until tender. Add the remaining ingredients and bring to a simmer. Cover and cook for 30 minutes. Add the fish and cook for another 20 minutes. Correct the seasonings if necessary and serve hot with a skillet of Mama's Cornbread. It's crusty on the outside and absolutely perfect!

Serves 6

Mama's Cornbread

1 cup white self-rising cornmeal
1/2 cup self-rising flour
1/2 teaspoon baking powder
1 egg
1 cup buttermilk
2 tablespoons vegetable oil

Preheat oven to 425° .
Combine all ingredients in a bowl and stir vigorously to blend. When the cornbread mixture is thoroughly blended, pour it into a hot 9–inch cast iron skillet with 1 tablespoon of extra oil rolled around in it to coat the bottom and sides. Put the skillet of corn bread immediately into the hot oven and bake for about 20 minutes or until nicely browned. Serve immediately and enjoy!

Serves 4 to 6

Notes

Salads

Barcelona Salad with Sautéed Catfish

2 tablespoons white vinegar
1 tablespoon dry sherry
1/2 teaspoon paprika
1/4 teaspoon sugar
4 catfish fillets
2 tablespoons olive oil
1 tablespoon minced fresh garlic
1/2 cup minced red onion
3/4 cup seeded and minced tomatoes
1/4 cup thinly sliced stuffed green olives

In a small bowl, mix the vinegar, sherry, paprika and sugar. Stir until the sugar dissolves. Set aside.

Wash the catfish fillets, cut in 1/2-inch pieces and pat dry. Heat the olive oil in a small skillet. Sauté the catfish fillets and the minced garlic for 3 to 4 minutes, stirring constantly. Put the cooked mixture into a bowl with the onions, tomatoes and olives and mix well. Add the vinegar mixture to the bowl and toss the salad to completely coat the fish and vegetables. Serve immediately, while it is warm, on a nest of shredded lettuce or chill and serve cold. The salad will hold refrigerated for 2 days.

Serves 4

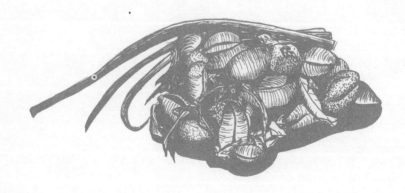

Green Bean and Corn Salad with Orange Catfish

1/4 cup vinegar
3 teaspoons coarse ground black pepper
2 tablespoons coarse mustard
2 teaspoons dried tarragon
1 tablespoon honey
3/4 cup vegetable oil
1 can Blue Lake whole green beans, drained
10-ounce package frozen whole kernel
   corn, thawed
1 cup thinly sliced green bell pepper
1/2 cup thinly sliced red onion
4 catfish fillets
1 cup orange juice
1 teaspoon orange zest

In a large bowl, mix the vinegar, pepper, mustard, honey, tarragon and oil, whisking well. Add the beans, corn, bell pepper and onion. Combine thoroughly. Set aside at room temperature, if you are serving the salad within hours. Or the salad may be made 2 to 3 days ahead, chilled and served cold. When you are ready to serve, wash the catfish fillets and pat dry. Put the orange juice and zest into a large skillet and bring to a simmer. Add the catfish fillets and poach for 5 to 6 minutes, turning if necessary. Serve immediately or refrigerate, if you plan to serve the salad cold.

On each plate, place several slices of fresh tomato. On top of the tomatoes, place one hot catfish fillet. Serve the prepared vegetable salad over the fillet, dividing evenly. Serve immediately.
Serves 4

Serve the salad at room temperature with the hot catfish one night, and both elements cold from the refrigerator for lunch 2 days later! We love having meals ready and waiting for busy days!

Eggplant Salad with Goat Cheese Croutons

1 medium eggplant
1/4 cup olive oil
2 tablespoons vinegar
2 cloves garlic, minced and crushed
1 tablespoon grated onion
2 tablespoons minced parsley
1 teaspoon oregano leaves
Salt and pepper to taste
1 large tomato, chopped
4 cooked catfish fillets, broiled, baked or
   poached
2 tablespoons chopped walnuts
Lemon wedges for garnish

Cut the eggplant in 1/2-inch thick slices and place them on a lightly oiled baking sheet. Broil the slices to a light brown on each side, watching them carefully. Cool and cut in 1 inch pieces.

In a small bowl, make a dressing with the oil, vinegar, garlic, onion, parsley and oregano, mixing well. Add salt and pepper to taste.

In a large bowl, combine the eggplant, tomatoes and the dressing, tossing carefully to coat. Adjust seasonings if needed. Chill before serving. The salad may be made 1 day ahead and the flavors do mellow nicely.

When you are ready to serve, place a catfish fillet on each plate, spoon the eggplant salad diagonally across the fish and sprinkle with the chopped walnuts. Serve with lemon wedges and the Goat Cheese Croutons.

Serves 4

Goat Cheese Croutons

Thin slices of French bread
(baguettes are best)
Butter to taste
Fresh soft goat cheese

Spread the thinly sliced bread with just a touch of butter. Spread each piece with goat cheese to suit your own taste. (I like a nice thick coating.) Broil for a minute or two to brown the edges of the bread and warm and toast the cheese.

Serve 1 or 100

The combination of flavors in this meal is particularly light and nice. And the Croutons are absolutely heavenly! Use these simple hot bread bites with a variety of main dishes. Or even as a quick pick up Hors d'Oeuvre when people drop in.

This salad is an excellent way to cook for two meals at once and PLAN for leftovers! The mild, sweet flavor of the catfish combines so nicely with the vinegary salad and the result is tasty, heart healthy and time efficient!

Lemon-Tarragon Catfish Salad

8 catfish fillets
1/3 cup vinegar
3/4 cup vegetable oil
2 cloves garlic, crushed
1 teaspoon dry mustard
1/2 teaspoon pepper
3/4 teaspoon salt
1/2 teaspoon chives
1/4 teaspoon basil
1/2 teaspoon parsley
1 cup mayonnaise
1 teaspoon dried tarragon
1 lemon rind, grated

Cut the catfish fillets into bite-size pieces. Make a marinade of the next 9 ingredients, blending thoroughly. Pour the mixture over the catfish pieces and set aside to marinate for at least one hour.

Drain the marinade and place the catfish pieces in a shallow pan. Bake for 20 minutes at 350°. Drain and cool the fish.

Meanwhile make a dressing with the mayonnaise, taragon and lemon peel, mixing well. When the fish is cool, gently-combine the fish and the lemon dressing. Refrigerate until ready to serve.

Serves 8

We serve the salad on a bed of lettuce, surrounded by fresh fruit and steamed, cold asparagus. With fresh hot bread, it is a perfect main dish salad. This dressing is rich and strong so other pronounced flavors are unnecessary. The salad also makes a great pick-up appetizer spooned onto triangles of toasted pita bread.

Suzanne Corder and I once served her Tarragon Chicken Salad, the inspiration for this catfish version, to a district Garden Club meeting in corsage boxes tied with ribbon—the perfect "box lunch," portable and pretty.

Louis-Style Catfish Salad

6 to 8 catfish fillets
3 teaspoons Old Bay Seasoning
4 cups water
1/2 cup mayonnaise
1/2 cup sour cream
2 tablespoons chili sauce
2 tablespoons salad oil
1 tablespoon white vinegar
1 tablespoon horseradish
1 tablespoon fresh lemon juice
1 tablespoon chopped parsley
2 teaspoons grated onion
1/2 teaspoon salt
4 drops Tabasco
Shredded lettuce
Hard boiled eggs, tomatoes and
  lemon to garnish

Wash the catfish fillets and cut in bite-size pieces. Place them in a saucepan with 4 cups water and the Old Bay Seasoning. Bring to a boil. Cut the heat off and let the catfish cool in the seasoned water. Refrigerate until needed, up to two days.

Make the Louis dressing by combining in a small bowl the remaining ingredients through the Tabasco. The sauce can be made ahead and refrigerated for up to 3 days.

When you are ready to serve, shred the lettuce onto a plate, pile the seasoned catfish on top of the lettuce and pour the Louis dressing over the fish. Garnish the plate with the eggs, sliced tomatoes and lemon.

Serves 6

The number of people you can serve with this recipe depends on the size of your servings. The catfish pieces are so good cooked this way that you will probably want large servings of the fish. And it holds so well refrigerated, that it's a great summer salad to deliberately make extra for "leftovers."

Oriental Catfish Salad

4 cooked catfish fillets, baked, broiled or
poached
1 cup thinly sliced cucumber
1 cup chopped fresh tomatoes
1/2 cup chopped green bell pepper
2 green onions, chopped
1 cup blanched snow peas (optional)
3 tablespoons soy sauce
5 tablespoons rice vinegar
1/2 teaspoon sugar
2 teaspoons sesame oil
3 teaspoons toasted sesame seeds

Flake the catfish and set aside. Cut all the vegetables and mix in a large bowl. Make the dressing by combining the soy sauce, vinegar, sugar and oil in a small bowl. Mix well to dissolve the sugar. Pour the dressing over the vegetables and toss to coat. Add the flaked catfish and sesame seeds, tossing carefully to combine thoroughly. The salad can be made ahead and refrigerated overnight, or it can be served immediately.

Serves 4

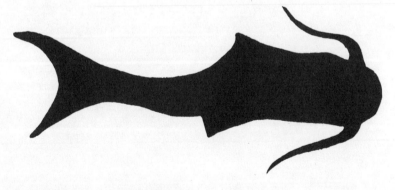

Serve this delightfully different salad as a main dish on a bed of lettuce leaves. Or serve it as a side salad with an omelet and some wonderful fresh bread. Calories are minimal and flavor is fabulous!

Rémoulade of Catfish

8 catfish fillets
3 cups water
2 teaspoons Old Bay Seasoning
2 bay leaves
1 cup mayonnaise
1/3 cup Creole Mustard
1/3 cup horseradish
1 tablespoon lemon juice
1 tablespoon Worcestershire sauce
3 drops Tabasco (or to taste)
1 tablespoon grated onion

Wash the catfish fillets and cut into bite-size pieces. Bring the water, bay leaves and Old Bay Seasoning to a boil. Reduce heat to a simmer. Add the catfish chunks and simmer until cooked. Cool in the cooking liquid.

Mix the remaining 7 ingredients for the Rémoulade Sauce in a glass bowl. Set aside. When the catfish has cooled, drain the pieces and gently stir them into the Rémoulade Sauce, coating the catfish thoroughly. Refrigerate. The Rémoulade Sauce should be made at least 24 hours before serving, but it can be made up to 3 days ahead.

Serves 20

This is one of those wonderful Louisiana dishes that can be made ahead and will just get better with time to marinate. Try using some shrimp (that is the traditional rémoulade) with the catfish for a nice texture and flavor change. Serve the rémoulade mounded on a platter of shredded lettuce for buffet service. For individual luncheon plates, serve on shredded lettuce garnished with tomato and boiled egg wedges.

Rice and Black Bean Salad with Broiled Catfish

6 cups chicken bouillon, divided
1 cup black beans
1 cup rice
1/2 cup each chopped green, red and
    yellow bell pepper
1/2 cup diced red onion
3 tablespoons chopped fresh cilantro
1/2 cup olive oil
1/4 cup orange juice
1 teaspoon grated orange rind
2 tablespoons vinegar
2 tablespoons red wine
1 teaspoon ground cumin
1 teaspoon chili powder
4 catfish fillets
Juice of 1 lemon
Sprinkling of chili powder
Lettuce leaves and lemon wedges
    to garnish each plate

In 3-3/4 cups of the chicken bouillon, cook the black beans until done, but still slightly crisp. In the remaining 2-1/4 cups of bouillon, cook the rice until done.

While the beans and rice are cooking, place the peppers, onion and cilantro in a large bowl. Make a dressing with the oil, juice, rind, vinegar, wine, cumin and 1 teaspoon of chili powder. Whisk together well and pour over the vegetables. Add the drained, cooked black beans and the cooked rice, while they are hot. Stir gently but thoroughly. Cover and keep slightly warm while the fish is cooking.

Wash the catfish fillets and cut in long strips. Pat dry. Place in a shallow pan and sprinkle with chili powder and the juice of 1 lemon. Broil, without turning, for 4 to 5 minutes. Serve the individual plates of warm Rice and Black Bean Salad topped with the hot broiled catfish. Garnish with lettuce leaves and lemon wedges. Serve immediately.

Serves 4

There will be some extra Rice and Black Bean Salad so plan to serve it cold within the next few days. With more catfish, or on its own! A satisfying and quite healthy main dish salad!

Stuffed Tomato with Catfish Salad

4 cooked catfish fillets, poached or baked
2 tablespoons mayonnaise
1 tablespoon fresh lemon juice
2 tablespoons sweet pickle relish
2 tablespoons chopped green olives
1 teaspoon prepared horseradish
2 green onions, minced
2 tablespoons minced onion
2 hard boiled eggs, finely chopped
1 teaspoon black pepper
Salt to taste
4 medium tomatoes

Flake the cooked catfish into a bowl. Add the remaining ingredients and mix thoroughly. Correct the seasonings with salt and more pepper to your own taste. Refrigerate until needed.

Core the tomato and cut in six wedges, leaving the bottom intact. Spread the wedges, like flower petals, and fill with the cold Catfish Salad. Garnish the top with paprika and green olive slices and serve on a bed of shredded lettuce. Refrigerate until ready to serve.

Serves 4

Add a hot cheese soufflé and fresh strawberries to the plate for a lovely summer luncheon. Or for a quick hot supper dish, cut a sweet, Vidalia onion in half, remove a bit of the center to create a cavity, cover and microwave for 6 minutes or until cooked. Fill the hot onion with the cold Catfish Salad and serve immediately—the flavors blend beautifully! Of course the salad makes great sandwiches on cold bread or the old fashioned way with cold salad between pieces of hot toasted bread!

Sunflower Slaw

**4 cooked catfish fillets, poached,
  broiled or baked
1 tablespoon vegetable oil
1 tablespoon fresh lemon juice
1 teaspoon sugar
3/4 teaspoon salt
2 tablespoons minced mint leaves
1 teaspoon minced celery leaves
2 tablespoons minced cilantro (optional)
1/3 cup thinly sliced onion
1/2 cup grated carrot
3 cups finely shredded cabbage
1/2 cup sunflower kernels to garnish**

In a small bowl, whisk together the oil, lemon juice, sugar, salt, mint leaves, celery leaves and cilantro. Set aside for a few minutes for the flavors to blend. Meanwhile, shred the cabbage and cut the onion and carrot. Toss the dressing with the vegetables to coat thoroughly. The salad may be prepared several hours early and refrigerated. It is best made the day it is to be used. The salad will still taste good 24 hours later, but will not be as crisp.

When you are ready to serve, divide most of the salad between the plates, reserving a cup or so in the bowl. Cut the cooked catfish in strips or chunks and add it to the bowl, tossing it with the reserved salad to coat. Divide the fish mixture between the plates, placing it on top of the first part. Serve immediately sprinkled with the sunflower kernels.

Serves 4

Crisp, nutritious and just faintly exotic in flavor. This main dish salad is excellent with warm pita bread, or toasted slices of French bread.

Pastas

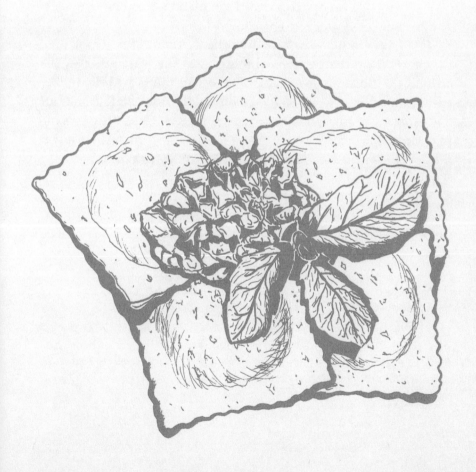

Fettucine with Catfish in Black Peppercorn Sauce

2 teaspoons butter
3 green onions, minced
2 teaspoons coarse ground black pepper
1/2 cup dry white wine
3 catfish fillets, cut in thin strips
3/4 cup milk
3/4 cup whipping cream
1/4 teaspoon nutmeg
1/2 teaspoon salt
1 teaspoon fresh lemon juice
8 ounces fettucine, cooked and drained
Chopped parsley or chives to garnish

In a heavy skillet, over medium heat, melt butter. Cook the onions and pepper for 1 minute. Add the wine and catfish strips, stirring gently to coat catfish on all sides. Add the milk, cream, nutmeg and salt, continuing to stir. Add the lemon juice and stir constantly while the sauce thickens. Check the seasonings and adjust if necessary. Serve immediately tossed with the fettucine. Sprinkle each serving with parsley or chives.

Serves 4

The peppercorn sauce is a bit hot—but it's a nice hot. Spicy and smooth. You can always cut down on the pepper, but try it this way first. A small serving makes a great first course, but with a nice spinach salad, the pasta makes a really satisfying, comforting main dish.

Lemon-Lime Catfish with Cold Pasta

4 catfish fillets
3 cups water
1 lemon, sliced
2 bay leaves
Juice of 2 lemons
Juice of 1 lime
8 ounces angel hair pasta
1/4 cup soy sauce
1 teaspoon oriental sesame oil
1/2 teaspoon sugar
2 tablespoons rice vinegar
1/2 cup diced cucumber
4 green onions, minced

Wash the catfish fillets and cut in 1/2-inch pieces. Bring the water to a simmer with the lemon slices and bay leaves. Add the catfish pieces, bring the water back to a slight simmer and cook for 10 minutes. Let the catfish cool in the broth. Drain the catfish pieces and cover them with the lemon and lime juice. This may be done several hours early and chilled.

Cook the pasta according to directions on the package. Drain and rinse until cold under running water. Drain again. Make a dressing of the soy sauce, sesame oil, sugar and rice vinegar. Be sure the sugar is well dissolved. Toss the pasta with the soy dressing. Add the cucumber and onion and continue to toss until it is well mixed. Add the reserved catfish pieces with the juices, mixing carefully and well. Serve immediately or refrigerate and serve within 24 hours.

Serve 4

This main dish pasta salad is light and delicious—but heart healthy as well. Serve with fresh fruit and fresh cold asparagus for a complete lunch or Southern summer supper.

Glazed Catfish Pasta with Artichoke-Mushroom Sauce

8 catfish fillets
2 cups flour
1 teaspoon salt
1 teaspoon black pepper
Oil for frying
1 pound spinach fettucine

Artichoke-Mushroom Sauce

1/2 cup butter
1/2 cup flour
1 cup minced onions
8 ounces sliced mushrooms
3 cloves garlic, crushed and minced
3 cups chicken broth
1/2 cup red wine
3 tablespoons chopped parsley
1/4 teaspoon thyme
1/4 teaspoon oregano
1/4 teaspoon cayenne pepper
1 16-ounce can artichokes,
   drained and chopped

To make the Artichoke-Mushroom Sauce, melt the butter in a heavy pan over low heat. Add the flour and cook the roux, stirring constantly, until it is a rich, chocolate brown. Add the onions, mushrooms and garlic. Continue to stir and cook until they are soft. Add the broth and red wine, stirring to blend thoroughly. Add the remaining ingredients and simmer slowly for another 10 minutes. The sauce may be made 2 days ahead and stored refrigerated until needed.

Wash the catfish fillets and cut in 1/2-inch pieces. Pat dry. Mix the flour, salt and pepper in a bowl. Dredge the catfish chunks in the flour mixture and fry in hot oil very briefly, do not let the catfish chunks brown. Remove and drain. Set aside while the rest of the chunks cook.

Cook the fettuccine al dente, or according to directions on the package. Drain the pasta and divide between individual au gratin dishes. Divide the catfish chunks over the pasta and cover the pieces of fish with the Artichoke-Mushroom Sauce. Place the dishes under the broiler for 5 to 6 minutes, until the catfish is heated through and the sauce is lightly glazed. Serve immediately. (If individual dishes are unavailable, glaze the catfish chunks under the broiler with the sauce, and then serve onto the plates of pasta.)

Serves 6 to 8

Serve this very rich dish with buttered fresh asparagus or broccoli, marinated tomatoes and a good hot bread. Wonderful! Also try this as a seated appetizer! Put just a few chunks of fish, without the pasta, in each dish and cover with the sauce. This can be made into small servings for a first course, and larger for an entree!

Levee Spaghetti Sauce

5 catfish fillets
1 tablespoon vegetable oil
2 onions, diced
1 green bell pepper, diced
1 can sliced tomatoes (28-ounce)
2 cans tomato paste (6-ounce)
1-1/2 cups water
2 teaspoons salt
1 teaspoon black pepper
1 teaspoon garlic powder
1 teaspoon sugar
2 bay leaves
12 ounces vermicelli
Grated Parmesan cheese

Wash the catfish fillets and cut in 1/2-inch pieces. In a large, heavy saucepan, heat the oil and add the catfish, onions and green pepper. Stir constantly until the onions are soft and the fish cooked. Add the remaining ingredients and mix well. Simmer the Levee Spaghetti Sauce for 1 to 2 hours. Correct seasonings and refrigerate until needed.

When you are ready to serve, cook the vermicelli according to directions on the package. Heat the Sauce and pour over the cooked pasta. Sprinkle with Parmesan cheese and serve immediately.

Serves 6 to 8

The Levee Spaghetti Sauce can be frozen for later use. And be sure to try the Overnight Lasagna using this sauce as well. If you don't want to make your own tomato sauce using this recipe, then simply heat some bought spaghetti sauce, add some small chunks of raw catfish and simmer the in the sauce until the fish is cooked. The juices from the fish will bind with the tomato sauce and you can throw in a few herbs to freshen the flavor of the prepared sauce. Not quite as good as homemade, but very quick!

Overnight Levee Lasagna

1 pound Ricotta cheese
1/2 pound shredded Mozzarella cheese
1 egg
1 teaspoon basil
1 recipe Levee Spaghetti Sauce
8 ounces uncooked lasagna noodles
1/2 cup water

In a bowl mix the Ricotta, egg, basil and all but 1/2 cup of the Mozzarella. Spread 1/2 cup of the Levee Spaghetti Sauce in a lightly buttered 9- by 13-inch baking pan. Top the sauce with a layer of the uncooked noodles, all of the cheese mixture and one-half the remaining sauce. Make a second layer of noodles, the rest of the sauce and the reserved 1/2 cup of Mozzarella. Pour the 1/2 cup of water around the edges of the pan and cover tightly with plastic wrap. Refrigerate overnight.

When you are ready to serve, remove the plastic wrap, cover with aluminum foil and bake at 350° for one hour. Let the Lasagna stand for 15 minutes before serving.

Serves 8

This recipe is crazy, but it really does work! It is fast, simple and tasty! Top with a dusting of Parmesan cheese just as it comes out of the oven!

Pasta with Catfish-Garlic Sauce

2 cooked catfish fillets, poached or broiled
2 tablespoons vegetable or olive oil
1/2 teaspoon garlic powder
1/4 teaspoon oregano leaves
1 tablespoon chopped parsley
1/8 teaspoon black pepper
Salt to taste
1/2 cup clam juice (or dry white wine)
Pasta of your choice (we like vermicelli)
Parmesan cheese

Dice the cooked catfish and set it aside. Heat the oil in a small skillet. Add the garlic, oregano, parsley, pepper and clam juice. Stir this mixture on low heat for 1 minute. Add the diced catfish and heat, stirring, for 1 to 2 minutes. Add salt to taste. (Salt will probably not be needed if you use clam juice, but it might if you use wine.) Set aside while you cook the pasta, but keep it warm. Place the servings of pasta onto the plates, pour the warm sauce over the pasta and serve immediately. Pass grated Parmesan cheese.

Serves 2

Plan this easy pasta dish for a busy, busy day. You've had no time to cook, but you did poach a few extra fillets the day before yesterday and they are cold and firm in the refrigerator waiting for you. This recipe won't take ten minutes to do. Throw together a fast green salad, heat a loaf of French bread, and they'll never know you were late getting home! But best of all— this is a very satisfying meal. I like large servings of pasta because the sauce is rich and strong. Enjoy!

Pasta with Mushrooms and Cream

4 catfish fillets
4 tablespoons butter
1 tablespoon olive oil
1/2 cup chopped green onions
1 clove garlic, minced
1/2 pound fresh mushrooms, sliced
2 tablespoons fresh lemon juice
1/4 cup dry white wine
1/2 cup whipping cream
2 teaspoons rosemary, crushed
1 tablespoon chopped fresh parsley
1/4 teaspoon black pepper
Salt to taste
1 pound fettucine or angel hair pasta

Wash catfish and pat dry. Cut into bite-size pieces and set aside.

Melt butter and oil in a heavy skillet. Add the green onions, garlic and mushrooms. Cook over medium heat until tender. Add the catfish pieces and stir gently for 1 to 2 minutes. Add the remaining ingredients and simmer the sauce for about 15 minutes, stirring constantly until thickened. The sauce will hold warm at this point for 30 to 45 minutes. Add more cream if the sauce is too thick.

Cook the pasta according to the package directions. Serve the warm sauce tossed with the pasta.

Serves 6

Ravioli with Roasted Yellow-Pepper Sauce

1 pound catfish fillets, diced
2 tablespoons butter
2 green onions, finely chopped
1 tablespoon lemon juice
1/2 teaspoon dried tarragon
2 tablespoons dry bread crumbs
2 egg yolks
1/8 teaspoon white pepper
1/4 teaspoon salt
WonTon wrappers, 1 package

Melt the butter in a heavy skillet and cook the green onions over medium heat for 1 minute, stirring. Add the diced catfish fillets and continue to stir until the fish is cooked, 2 to 3 minutes. Place the mixture in a bowl. Add the remaining ingredients, stirring thoroughly to mix the flavors and mash the fish. Refrigerate until chilled. This can be prepared a day ahead.

Place 1 wonton wrapper on a lightly floured surface, brush the edges with water. Place 1 tablespoon filling in the middle of the wrapper. Put another wrapper on top of the first and seal the edges, being careful to remove as much air inside the ravioli as possible. Continue to make the ravioli, placing them on a kitchen towel to dry slightly.

Place the filled ravioli in a pan of gently boiling water, a few at a time. Cook for 2 to 3 minutes. Remove them with a slotted spoon and drain on kitchen towels. Keep warm.

Serves 6

Roasted Yellow-Pepper Sauce

2 large yellow (or red) peppers
2 cloves minced garlic
2 tablespoons olive oil
Salt to taste

Roast the peppers by placing cut halves under the broiler and cook until skin is blackened. Watch closely. Peel the skin from the peppers and chop the meat coarsely. Sauté peppers and garlic in olive oil for 2 to 3 minutes. Place this mixture in a processor and puree. Keep warm to serve with the ravioli.

Makes 2 cups

Serve the ravioli with the Yellow Pepper Sauce or use your imagination! A light cream sauce with a dusting of Parmesan cheese is easy and very good. Or serve over a bed of steamed fresh spinach and dust with cheese.

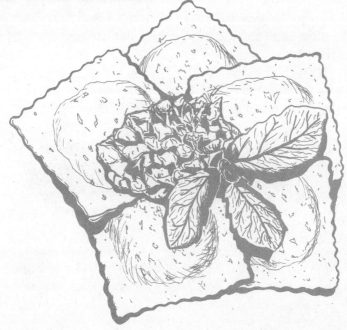

Pasta Salad with SMOKED CATFISH

1/3 cup vegetable or olive oil
2 green onions, finely chopped
3 tablespoons lemon juice
2 teaspoons dried dill weed
Salt to taste
Coarse ground black pepper to taste
8 ounces fusilli
   (or other fancy-shaped pasta)
2 SMOKED CATFISH FILLETS
   (available in specialty food stores or by mail order—see index)
3 tablespoons chopped chives
2 fresh tomatoes, chopped

Combine first 6 ingredients in a small bowl. Whisk dressing well and set aside. Cook the pasta in rapidly boiling water until just barely cooked. Drain well and rinse thoroughly under cold water. Place the pasta in a large bowl. Add the dressing and mix gently, but thoroughly.

Cut the SMOKED CATFISH diagonally across the fillet in thin strips. Mix the catfish strips, tomatoes and chives with the pasta, tossing carefully. Garnish with sour cream topped with fresh chives.

Serves 6 to 8

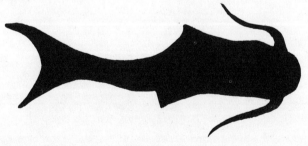

This salad is delicious as soon as it is made, but remember that pasta salads definitely develop flavor if they can sit overnight in the refrigerator. Served with crusty French bread, this main dish salad is perfect for hot weather meals.

Savory Catfish with Angel Hair Pasta

6 catfish fillets
2 teaspoons bottled horseradish
2 teaspoons grated fresh ginger
1/2 teaspoon sesame oil
2 tablespoons soy sauce
1-1/2 cups dry white wine
1/2 cup chopped green onions
12 ounces angel hair pasta
1 green onion, minced for garnish

Wash the catfish fillets and pat dry. Set aside on absorbent paper. Mix the horseradish, ginger, sesame oil, soy sauce, wine and green onions in a large skillet and blend well. Place the fillets in the skillet and marinate for at least 1 hour.

When you are ready to serve, bring the catfish and marinade to a simmer over medium heat and cook for 4 to 6 minutes, turning the fish once if it is too thick to be covered in the marinade. Set aside and keep warm.

Cook the pasta according to directions on the package—just barely done is best. Bring the fish back to a slight simmer. Serve the hot pasta onto the plates and ladle the fish fillet, some of the sauce, and a sprinkle of green onions over each serving.

Serves 6

Another low-fat entree—but it is so unbelievably good, no one would object to the calories! Serve a nice soup or salad first and then just a soft, fresh bread with the delicious pasta. The catfish dish is so light, this is a good time to splurge on dessert!

SMOKED CATFISH Fettucine with Yogurt-Dill Sauce

6 SMOKED CATFISH FILLETS
(available at specialty food stores or by mail order—see index)
12 ounces fettucine
1 cup plain non-fat yogurt
2 tablespoons coarse mustard
1 teaspoon dill
Pinch of sugar, if desired
1/2 teaspoon fresh lemon juice
1 clove garlic, minced and crushed

Mix the yogurt, mustard, dill, sugar, lemon juice and garlic in a small bowl. Set aside. This may be done the day before serving. Just before serving, heat the sauce carefully in a bowl of warm water—be careful not to get it hot enough to seprate.

Warm the SMOKED CATFISH FILLETS carefully in microwave, or gently in a conventional oven. They are already fully cooked. Keep warm.

Cook the fettucini according to directions on the package. Do not overcook. Drain well and divide the hot pasta onto the serving plates. Place a SMOKED CATFISH FILLET on top of the pasta and cover with the Yogurt-Dill Sauce. Serve immediately.

Serves 6

Kitchen Delights in Jackson, Mississippi, has been serving our SMOKED CATFISH FILLETS on their changing monthly menu for several years. Cherry Dean was kind enough to share her secret recipe with us. We appreciate her generosity.

Entrees

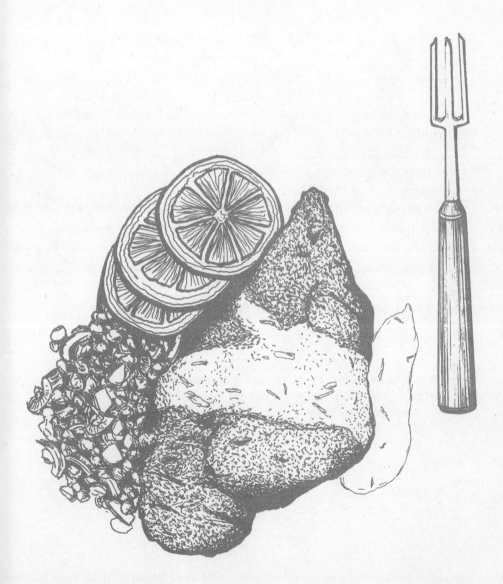

Catfish Allison

6 to 8 catfish fillets
1 cup grated Parmesan cheese
1/2 cup butter or margarine, softened
6 tablespoons mayonnaise
6 green onions, chopped fine
1/2 teaspoon Worcestershire sauce
Generous dash Tabasco

Place the cheese, butter, mayonnaise onion, Worcestershire and Tabasco in a bowl and mix thoroughly. Butter mixture may be made 24 hours ahead and kept refrigerated.

Poach the catfish fillets in lightly simmering water for 4 to 5 minutes. Gently lift the fillets from the water and set aside to drain.

For individual servings, place the fillets in au gratin dishes and cover with 2 tablespoons of the cheese mixture. Broil for 2 to 3 minutes until the cheese mixture browns.

Without individual dishes, place fillets into a lightly baking dish. Cover each fillet with the cheese mixture and brown under the broiler. Carefully lift the fillets from the dish onto the plates and spoon some of the pan juices over each serving.

Serves 6 to 8

Claudia Ainsworth shared this recipe, named for her daughter, with us years ago. It has become a favorite at THE CROWN because the sauce is so rich and good, you just have to capture every drop of it. Bill and Claudia were willing and wonderful food tasters during the writing of this cookbook! And our families have shared many special meals together over the years!

Apricot-Mustard Crusted Catfish

4 catfish fillets
2 tablespoons apricot jam
1 tablespoon Dijon mustard
1/4 cup grated Parmesan cheese
1 cup fine fresh bread crumbs

Combine the jam, mustard and cheese in a small bowl. Wash and pat dry the catfish fillets. Spread the mustard mixture on both sides of the fillets. Cover each fillet with fine bread crumbs. Place in a lightly buttered baking dish. Recipe may be prepared to this point and held refrigerated until needed.

When ready to serve, place the baking dish in a preheated 350° oven for about 20 minutes. Serve immediately.

Serves 4

If the weather is hot and you don't want to heat your oven, saute the fillets on top of the stove with a little butter in the skillet. You'll get a lovely result—it just takes a little more tending to. I like to serve this with sauteed fresh squash. For the best results, you must use butter, not margarine. It only takes a LITTLE butter and the taste is worth the calories!

Zucchini Sauté

1 cup sliced zucchini
1 cup sliced yellow squash
1 carrot, thinly sliced and blanched(optional)
1 tablespoon butter
1 teaspoon chopped parsley
Salt to taste

Melt the butter in a skillet over medium heat. Add the zucchini, squash and carrots, stirring constantly. Cook until just barely tender, 2 to 3 minutes. Add parsley and salt. Mix well and serve immediately.

Serves 4

Asparagus and Catfish Rolls

4 to 6 catfish fillets
2 tablespoons butter
2 tablespoons flour
1 cup milk
1 tablespoon lemon juice
1/2 teaspoon dry mustard
1/2 teaspoon garlic powder
Salt and pepper to taste
4 spears of asparagus per fillet
3 to 4 tablespoons Dijon mustard
4 to 6 tablespoons grated Parmesan cheese
1 cup soft bread crumbs
Lemon wedges for garnish

Wash the catfish fillets and pat dry. Wrap in kitchen towel or absorbent paper until needed.

Melt the butter in a heavy saucepan, stir in the flour and cook slowly for 2 to 3 minutes. Add the milk, stirring constantly until the sauce has thickened. Add the lemon juice, mustard and garlic. Salt and pepper to taste. Set the white sauce aside.

Cook fresh asparagus in gently simmering water until it is nearly done. Drain well. Or drain canned asparagus. Place one catfish fillet on a plate, spread with 1/2 tablespoon of Dijon mustard and 1 tablespoon of the white sauce. Place 4 spears of asparagus across the fillet, and gently roll the fish around the asparagus. Secure with a wooden pick. Place each roll in a lightly buttered baking dish. Cover each roll with 1 tablespoon of the white sauce, 1 tablespoon of Parmesan cheese and the soft bread crumbs. This recipe may be prepared ahead to this point and refrigerated until ready to use.

Bake uncovered in a preheated 350° oven for about 25 minutes. The crumb covering may need to be patted back onto the roll before serving. Dust with paprika and serve immediately with a wedge of lemon.

Serves 4 to 6

Perfect for a bridge luncheon! Light and delicious with a fresh fruit salad, tomato aspic and hot homemade rolls. Of course, the fresh asparagus makes a prettier, tastier dish, but when fresh is out of season, canned asparagus is an acceptable substitute.

Baked Catfish with Ratatouille

8 catfish fillets
1 large onion, diced
2 medium green bell peppers, diced
1/3 cup olive oil
3 medium eggplants, diced
16-ounce can tomatoes, with liquid
1 cup quartered and sliced yellow squash
1 tablespoon sugar
1/2 cup ketchup
2 tablespoons Worcestershire sauce
1-1/2 teaspoons salt
3 tablespoons dry red wine

Cook onion and green peppers in olive oil in a large heavy saucepan over medium heat until golden, stirring constantly. Add the eggplant and cook for another 15 minutes, continuing to stir. Add remaining ingredients, except catfish, and simmer for about 30 minutes, stirring occasionally. The sauce may be made ahead to this point and held, refrigerated, for up to 3 days or frozen until needed.

When ready to serve, wash the catfish fillets and pat dry. Place the fillets in an ungreased baking dish. Cover them generously with the sauce and bake in a preheated 350° oven for about 20 minutes. Serve immediately with any pan juices from the baking dish poured over the fillets.

Serves 8

I love a dish that is truly versatile—and this one is! The sauce makes a fabulous chafing dish dip with toasted pita bites or melba toast. It freezes perfectly, so you can prepare our wonderful catfish dish for 2 or 8 and plan on "leftover" sauce going into the freezer for another occasion. Or the other way around! So many dips, hot and cold, can be used as sauces for main dishes and enjoyed on another level. Be creative! You may never be able to duplicate the dish you enjoyed with the "leftovers," but your meals will not be boring!

Barbecued Catfish
New Orleans Style

4 to 6 catfish fillets
1/2 cup butter
1/2 cup olive or vegetable oil
1 teaspoon garlic powder
2 bay leaves
1 tablespoon chopped parsley
1/2 teaspoon oregano
2 teaspoons paprika
2 tablespoons Tabasco
1 tablespoon Worcestershire sauce
1 teaspoon salt
1 teaspoon black pepper
Juice of 2 lemons

Wash the catfish fillets. Cut into 1-inch pieces and set aside on absorbent paper.

Melt the butter in a large saucepan. Add oil and remaining ingredients, mixing well. Set aside for a few minutes for the flavors to blend or you can refrigerate the mixture overnight. When you are ready to serve, bring the butter mixture almost to a boil, add the catfish chunks and bring the mixture back to a simmer. Cook on low heat for about 15 minutes. Serve immediately in bowls with rice and good, crusty bread for dipping up the zesty sauce.

Serves 4

This classic Louisiana shrimp dish really translates well to catfish. Try mixing a few shrimp with the catfish—it will make the sauce even more rich and wonderful. We like to serve a good green salad before we dish up the Barbecued Catfish!

THE CROWN's
Blackened Catfish

6 catfish fillets
1/2 teaspoon garlic powder
1 teaspoon cayenne pepper
1 teaspoon black pepper
1 teaspoon salt
1 tablespoon crushed dried thyme leaves
1/2 teaspoon paprika
1 stick butter
Juice of 1 lemon
1/4 cup dry white wine

Wash the catfish fillets and pat dry. Set aside.

Combine all the dry ingredients in a small bowl and set aside. This can be mixed ahead of time, placed in a glass jar with a tight fitting lid and kept for months.

Melt the butter in a pan. Add the lemon juice and mix well. Dip the fillets into the butter mixture. Sprinkle the fillets liberally with the spice mixture, on both sides, and set aside.

When ready to serve, heat a black iron skillet on the stove until it is VERY hot! (It is always recommended to cook this outside because it will smoke a lot! But with a good vent, you can do it inside.) When you are sure the skillet is hot, carefully place the fillets in the skillet and cook them for about 2 minutes on each side. I keep them moving with a spatula, so they don't stick too badly. When the fillets are cooked, remove them from the skillet and remove the skillet from the hot burner. Pour the butter mixture into the skillet, quickly adding the wine and stir madly. Pour these pan juices over the fillets and serve immediately.

Serves 6

The spice mixture is really nice to have on hand, so double or triple it and store the extra. It's also a great way to do steaks (if you like them rare) or boneless chicken breasts.

Black Butter Catfish

6 farm-raised catfish fillets
1/2 cup butter
2 tablespoons white vinegar
2 tablespoons chopped pecans
  or sliced almonds

Poach the catfish fillets for 6 to 8 minutes in barely simmering water to which you have added a touch of white wine and 2 lemon slices. Lift the fillets carefully onto a plate to drain. The fillets will hold at this point, tightly covered in the refrigerator, for up to 24 hours.

For the Black Butter:

Place the butter in a heavy skillet and heat until it begins to color slightly. At this point, add the pecans or almonds and carefully stir to spread evenly over the skillet. Continue to stir, while the butter deepens to a rich, nutty brown and the nuts color. When the butter has ALMOST burned, slowly add the vinegar and STEP BACK. The steam and sizzle can scald. Take the skillet off the heat, stirring to let the foam subside. Set aside until needed. To serve, place poached fillets in individual serving dishes or a baking dish to hold them in one layer. Cover the fillets with the black butter, being sure to place the nuts on top of the fish. Heat for 10 to 15 minutes in 350° oven or until the butter sizzles in the dish. Serve with a wedge of lemon.

Serves 6

We were first served this wonderful butter on the Normandy coast years ago. The small family-owned hotel where we were staying was almost empty so early in the season, and we spent many lovely hours visiting with the owner and talking food and cooking. She served this butter with skate, a truly unattractive fish, but we have used it on everything imaginable. It can be refrigerated for a week and served over green beans, asparagus, broccoli or even sautéed chicken breasts.

Black Butter Catfish has been the all time favorite entree at THE CROWN since it opened in 1976. We explain that it isn't blackened with pepper, but has a rich, nutty flavor of it's own.

Broiled Catfish with Chive Butter

6 catfish fillets
Salt and pepper, to taste
1/2 cup butter
1 teaspoon minced parsley
1 tablespoon fresh lemon juice
1/4 teaspoon salt
1 tablespoon chives
1/8 teaspoon cayenne pepper

Wash the catfish fillets and pat dry. Place the fillets in a very lightly buttered baking dish, just large enough to hold them in one layer. Salt and pepper the fillets only slightly. We like lots of pepper but almost no salt. Set aside.

Melt the butter in a small saucepan and combine the remaining ingredients in the same pan. Rub each fillet with just a bit of the butter mixture. Broil the fish for about 5 minutes, without turning the fish over. Turn the broiler off and remove the pan from the oven. Cover each fillet with more of the chive butter and return the pan to the oven until you are ready to serve.

Serve the fillet over rice or pasta, with spoonfuls of the wonderful sauce from the pan.

Serves 6

The flavor of the chive butter is really exceptional in this dish, because the catfish itself is so mild and sweet. No fishy flavors to overcome! The butter can be made and refrigerated ahead of time, so this can become a ten-minute meal! And so good!

Chili Catfish Pie

1-1/2 cups cooked catfish, baked,
   broiled or poached
1/2 cup milk
2 tablespoons all-purpose flour
1/2 cup mayonnaise
2 eggs, beaten
1/3 cup chopped green onions
1 tablespoon chopped parsley
1 small can chopped green chilies,
   undrained
2 cups grated cheddar cheese
1/2 teaspoon salt
1 9-inch pastry shell

Preheat oven to 350° and bake the pie shell for 7 to 8 minutes.

Cut the cooked catfish into small pieces. Combine catfish and remaining ingredients in a bowl and mix thoroughly. Pour into the cooked pie shell. Bake for 1 hour. Serve immediately.

Serves 6

An excellent way to use leftover catfish! This is a convenient and very easy, main dish pie. It will even freeze! Serve it with a cup of soup in the winter or a green salad in the summer.

Catfish CICERO

6 catfish fillets
1 cup bread crumbs
1 cup Parmesan cheese
2/3 cup chopped parsley
1 cup chopped pecans
1 teaspoon oregano
1 tablespoon seasoned salt
1 beaten egg

Wash the catfish fillets and pat dry. Set aside. In a bowl, mix the bread crumbs, cheese, parsley, pecans, oregano and salt. Dip the fish into the beaten egg and then into the bread crumb mixture, coating the fish thoroughly. Place the fillets in oiled ramekins or on an oiled baking sheet. Bake for 18 to 20 minutes in a 450° to 500° oven. Serve immediately.

Serves 6

CICERO's Restaurant on Deer Creek, just out of Leland, Mississippi, is a favorite of locals and visitors to the Stoneville Experiment Station. Becky Walker says one of their customers called Catfish CICERO, "Catfish with a tuxedo on." And you'll agree with us that this recipe is good! At CICERO's, the catfish dishes, and everything else on the menu, are prepared for you as though you were a guest in the Walker's home. That's called Southern hospitality!

Citrus Butter Catfish

4 to 6 catfish fillets
1/2 cup dry white wine
1/4 cup fresh orange juice
1/2 teaspoon orange zest
5 tablespoons butter
1 teaspoon lemon juice
1/4 teaspoon salt
1/8 teaspoon white pepper
1 teaspoon minced chives

Cut each fillet lengthwise into 2 pieces. Wash and pat dry. Melt 1 tablespoon butter in a heavy skillet. Sauté the catfish pieces, a few at a time, over medium heat until done, 2 to 3 minutes. Add more butter as needed. Keep catfish pieces warm. To the same pan add the wine, juice and zest, scraping the bottom of the pan with a wooden spoon. Cook rapidly to reduce the sauce to 1/2 cup. Remove from heat and slowly beat in the remaining 3 tablespoons of butter, 1 tablespoon at a time. The sauce should thicken slightly. Add the lemon juice, salt, pepper and chives. Mix well. Pour the sauce over the sautéed catfish.

Serves 4 to 6

The sauce is rich and very flavorful, best served with lightly buttered new potatoes and a fresh green vegetable. A lovely presentation would be freshly cooked crêpes enclosing the sauced fillets with a bit more sauce over the crêpe. Garnish with fresh orange slices.

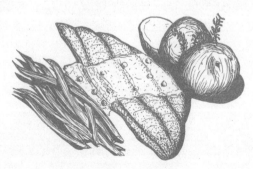

Corn and Catfish Casserole

Sliced French bread, toasted
4 catfish fillets
2 ears fresh corn OR 1 16-ounce can
whole kernel corn, drained
1-1/2 cups milk
3 eggs
1/2 cup minced onion
1/2 cup minced green bell pepper
1/2 cup minced red bell pepper
1/2 teaspoon salt
1 tablespoon Worcestershire sauce
2 teaspoons prepared mustard
1/2 teaspoon white pepper

Preheat oven to 325°.

Toast enough slices of French bread to cover the bottom of a buttered 2-quart casserole. Line the casserole with the toasted bread.

Wash the catfish fillets and cut in 1-inch chunks. Place the catfish chunks over the bread in one layer. Set aside. Scrape the fresh corn and all the juices into a bowl. Add the remaining ingredients and mix thoroughly. Pour the corn mixture over the fish. Cover the casserole loosely with foil. Bake for 1 hour or until set.

Serves 4 to 6

This variation of a Charleston shrimp and corn pie is a wonderful Sunday night supper. You can put the shrimp back into the recipe, of course, but it is healthier this way. Or try it with leftover bits of ham (and leave out the salt). It's a good recipe for changing to suit your personal tastes and what's in your refrigerator at the moment!

Cornmeal Catfish Bake

1 cup self-rising cornmeal
1/2 cup self-rising flour
1/2 teaspoon baking powder
1 egg
1 cup buttermilk
2 tablespoons salad oil
8 catfish fillets
Paprika
3 tablespoons butter
1-1/2 cups chopped green onions
1/2 teaspoon salt
1/4 teaspoon pepper
1 tablespoon lemon juice
1 tablespoon flour
1 cup sour cream

Preheat oven to 375°. Place the first 6 ingredients in a small bowl and stir vigorously to mix. Pour the cornbread mixture into a well-buttered 9- by 13-inch glass baking dish. Spread evenly.

Wash the catfish fillets and cut each one into 3 parts. Cover the cornbread mixture with a layer of the catfish fillets. Dust the fillets generously with paprika.

Melt the butter in a small skillet. Add the green onion and cook over medium heat for 3 to 4 minutes until soft. Remove from heat. Add the next 5 ingredients and mix thoroughly. Pour this sour cream topping over the catfish layer. Spread it carefully to completely cover the dish.

Bake for 40 to 45 minutes. The cornbread layer should be nicely browned and the topping soft. Serve immediately.

Serves 8

Serve the Cornmeal Bake with a Tomato Salsa for an added touch of flavor and color. This is a great do-ahead dish. It reheats beautifully and will even freeze—so leftovers can be a busy day bonus.

Dill-Baked Catfish with Yogurt-Lemon Sauce

6 catfish fillets
4 green onions, cut in 1/2-inch pieces
2 teaspoons dried dill weed
2 lemons, sliced
1 teaspoon coarse ground black pepper
Salt to taste
1 teaspoon butter or margarine

Lightly butter a baking dish that will just hold the fish fillets. Place the lemon slices on the bottom of the dish. Top with the green onion slices and sprinkle with the dill weed. Place the fish on top and season with salt and pepper. Cover very tightly with foil or tight fitting lid so that the fish will steam.

Preheat the oven to 350° and bake for about 20 minutes. Serve immediately with the pan juices spooned over each serving. Pass the sauce separately.

Serves 6

Yogurt-Lemon Sauce

1 cup plain yogurt
1 large garlic clove, minced
Juice of 1 lemon
1 green onion, finely chopped
1 teaspoon dried dill weed
Salt to taste
1/2 teaspoon white pepper

Mix all ingredients in a glass bowl and set aside. Sauce can be made a day ahead and refrigerated.

Makes 1 cup

This is an easy recipe to adjust to serve 2 or 20, and so easy to prepare. Low in fat and calories, but high in flavor and freshness.

Dilled Catfish McElmurray

6 catfish fillets
1/4 cup fresh lime juice
1 teaspoon dill weed
1 clove garlic, minced
Salt and pepper, to taste

Wash the catfish fillets and pat dry. Squeeze the lime juice over the fish and let it marinate at least 30 minutes in the refrigerator. Grease a shallow baking pan, just large enough to hold the fish in one layer, with margarine. Put the fish fillets into the pan and sprinkle with the dill, garlic, salt and pepper. Bake in a preheated 350° oven for 5 to 10 minutes, or until the fish flakes easily. Serve immediately with a wedge of lime to garnish.

Serves 6

Lori McElmurray, a young cousin who is a Nutrition major at Mississippi State University, worked with this recipe in a Food Laboratory project. She prepared it for 130 people, serving them 115 calories per catfish fillet with only 4 grams of saturated fat. Another good example of the nutritional excellence of catfish!

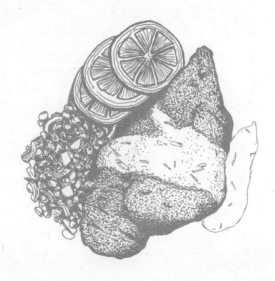

Elizabethan Catfish

3 ounces Mozzarella cheese, grated
3 ounces Swiss cheese, grated
1/2 cup finely chopped mushrooms
2 tablespoons finely chopped green onions
2 cloves garlic, minced
1/2 teaspoon black pepper
6 to 8 catfish fillets
1 tablespoon white wine per fillet

Preheat oven to 350°. Lightly butter a baking dish to hold the fillets without crowding. Wash the fillets, pat dry and place in the baking dish.

Mix the cheeses, mushrooms, onions, garlic and pepper, combining well. Divide the cheese mixture evenly on the fillets, mounding and pressing the cheese onto the fillet. Drizzle the wine over each fillet. Bake for 20 minutes uncovered. Place under a broiler for a few minutes to toast the cheese topping. Serve immediately with the pan juices spooned over the fish.

Serves 6 to 8

How easy can you get? And the look and flavor are great! We've been doing an Elizabethan Steak for years at THE CROWN. In fact, it was the first entree we offered when THE CROWN was opened for evening parties. Our patient editor, Martha Weeks, who willingly sampled multitudes of catfish dishes with us while this book was in progress, especially likes the Elizabethan Steak. She suggested we try the same stuffing with catfish! And it is delicious!

If you want to try the steak version, use 1-inch rib-eye steaks, cut a pocket for the stuffing, splash them with Worcestershire sauce, fresh lemon juice and lots of pepper. Broil to your liking and serve with any juices that accumulate. Scrumptious!

English Fish and Chips

8 catfish fillets
2 cups flour, divided
1-1/2 teaspoons salt, divided
1 cup cold water
2 tablespoons vegetable oil
1 teaspoon baking powder
Peanut oil for frying
2 to 3 large potatoes

Peel the potatoes. Cut into slices, then into strips. Drop them into cold water, and set aside until needed.

Wash the catfish fillets and pat dry. Mix 1 cup flour with 1/2 teaspoon salt. Dredge the fillets in this mixture one at a time. Set aside.

For the batter, combine the water, corn oil and 1 teaspoon salt in a bowl. Add 1 cup flour, gradually, whisking to prevent lumps. Just before dipping the fish, add the baking powder, whisking to blend.

Dip the floured fillets, one at a time, into the batter. Drop them into the hot peanut oil. Turn the fillets as they cook. They will be puffed and browned in 1-1/2 to 2 minutes. Remove and drain. Continue frying until all the fish are cooked. Drain the cut potatoes and pat dry. Heat the oil to a higher temperature for the potatoes and cook them a few at a time. Remove and drain. Serve immediately.

Serves 8

Now, to be perfectly authentic and serve Fish and Chips like they do in England—a few extra touches are needed. Malt vinegar and salt should be sprinkled onto the fish and chips before rolling them up in newspaper to keep warm. The chips and the fish have to be piled in the paper together so that they stick to each other and the batter comes off the fish when picking up a chip. Somehow, eating fish and chips with your fingers from the newspaper with a can of warm cola to drink is a feeling you can't duplicate, no matter how right the batter is! You need to stand in line at the fish and chips shop, order your "plaice and chips—twice," and go out into the damp, cool English evening. The catfish translates well for the plaice—but can your kitchen ever become that English roadside?

Frittered Catfish Kabobs
(Fish on a Stick)

4 catfish fillets
1 onion
Sliced dill pickles
1-1/2 cups all-purpose flour
1-1/4 cups milk
2 egg yolks
1 teaspoon salt
1/2 teaspoon pepper
1 teaspoon chili powder
1 teaspoon oregano
8 wooden skewers (4-inch)
Peanut oil for deep frying

Wash the catfish. Cut the fillets into 1-inch pieces and set aside on absorbent paper. Cut the onion in 1- to 1-1/2-inch pieces. Using short (4-inch) wooden skewers, alternately thread pieces of catfish, onion and dill pickle onto each skewer, filling them fairly close to the ends. Place a piece of onion on each end.

Make a batter with the flour, milk, egg yolks and seasonings, mixing gently, but well. Try to allow time for the batter to mellow in the refrigerator, even overnight. You can use the batter immediately if you are in a hurry, but the resting just makes it better.

When you are ready to serve, heat the oil to the correct temperature, approximately 375°. You can test the temperature by dropping a cube of bread into the hot oil—if it browns in 60 seconds, the oil is ready.

Dip the Catfish Kabobs in the batter, being sure that all the surfaces are covered. Immediately place the Kabobs in the hot oil, one or two at a time. Cook until nicely browned, remove immediately, drain and keep warm while the rest are cooking.

Fills 8 skewers—Serving 4

Don't waste the extra batter. Use all those bits of onion that wouldn't go onto the skewer, a few more dill pickles and fry those too! The batter will hold for 24 hours, but the oil is hot now. The fried dill pickles are a tradition in parts of the Mississippi Delta!

Florentine Catfish

6 to 8 catfish fillets
3 cups water
1 lemon, sliced
10-ounce package frozen, chopped spinach
4 tablespoons butter
1 clove garlic, minced
3 green onions, finely chopped
4 tablespoons flour
2 cups milk
1/2 teaspoon dry mustard
1/2 teaspoon white pepper
1 teaspoon salt
3 teaspoons lemon juice
1 cup grated Swiss cheese, divided

In a large saucepan, bring the water and lemon slices to a slow simmer. Add the catfish fillets and poach gently for about 8 minutes. Remove fillets and drain well.

Thaw and drain the spinach. Place it in a kitchen towel and squeeze the moisture from the spinach. Set aside.

Melt butter in a heavy saucepan. Add green onions and garlic. Cook briefly to soften. Add flour and stir constantly while the roux cooks. Do not brown. Slowly add the milk, continuing to stir until the sauce is smooth and thickened. Add reserved spinach, seasonings, lemon juice and 1/2 cup of the cheese, mixing well.

The sauce may be prepared ahead to this point and refrigerated until needed, up to 2 days.

When you are ready to serve, place the cooked catfish fillets in a lightly buttered 9- by 13-inch baking dish or individual au gratin dishes. Cover with sauce and top with remaining cheese. Bake at 350° for 15 minutes or until bubbly. Finish under the broiler to lightly toast the cheese. Serve immediately.

Serves 6 to 8

*When company's coming, this is a great dish
to prepare because all the work is done ahead of
time. You can refrigerate the fish in its baking dish
and pop it into the oven at the last minute. Serve with
buttered new potatoes and crisp Vegetable Vinaigrette.*

Vegetable Vinaigrette

**1 cup good salad oil
1/3 cup white vinegar
2 teaspoons crushed oregano leaves
1 teaspoon salt
1/2 teaspoon coarse ground black pepper
1/2 teaspoon dry mustard
2 cloves garlic, crushed
2 tablespoons finely minced onion,
2 tablespoons minced fresh parsley**

Combine all ingredients in a jar with a top. Shake well to
blend. Set aside. Prepare the vegetables you wish to marinate.
Cut tomatoes in 1/2-inch slices. Fresh asparagus should be
blanched, rinsed and drained. Zucchini and yellow squash
should be thinly sliced. Cut cucumbers in 1/4-inch slices.
Green beans should be left whole, blanched and dunked in ice
water. New potatoes should be cooked al dente and cut in 1/2-
inch slices. Just use your imagination—guided by what is available in your fresh food market.

Cover prepared vegetables with vinaigrette and refrigerate
for at least 3 hours or up to 24 hours.

Makes 1-1/2 cups

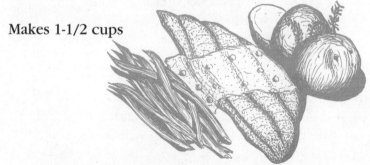

Fried Catfish and Hushpuppies

4 to 6 catfish fillets
Buttermilk
Salt and pepper
White corn meal
Peanut or vegetable oil to fry

Wash the catfish fillets and pat dry. Place the fillets in a shallow pan and pour about 2 tablespoons of buttermilk over each. Rub the milk into the fish, and then turn the fillet over in the pan to coat the other side with the milk.

Lightly salt the fish, but sprinkle the pepper generously! Pour approximately 2 cups of corn meal into a bag or a deep bowl. Place the fillets, one at a time, into the corn meal and shake the bag or bowl, covering the fish thoroughly with meal.

Heat the oil to approximately 375° and fry the fish until lightly browned. Do not crowd the fish. To hold the cooked fish while the rest are frying, place the cooked fillets in a brown paper bag and close tightly. Serve immediately with Hushpuppies and fried potatoes cooked in the same hot oil. You also have to serve Coleslaw and ketchup for the perfect Delta Fish Fry!

Serves 4

Mama's Hushpuppies

1 cup white self-rising corn meal
4 green onions, chopped
1 teaspoon black pepper
1/2 cup milk

Mix the corn meal, onions and pepper in a small bowl. Add the milk and mix thoroughly. Make sure that the oil is hot and ready. Using a teaspoon, scoop out a rounded spoonful of hushpuppy batter. Lightly roll and mash it against the side of the bowl on one side and then the other. This will compress the mixture slightly and prevent the hushpuppy from falling apart in the hot oil. Using another teaspoon, push the hushpuppy off the spoon into the hot oil. Work quickly to fry 6 or 8 at a time, but do not crowd them. Fry until they are browned and serve immediately. Absolutely delicious and just enough for four!

Serves 4

The number of people you can serve at a fish fry really depends on the amount they eat! I always count on 2 pieces of fish per person, (or more if there are lots of boys) because you want to fry the smaller fillets if possible. You will want to cut the larger fillets in half diagonally—they just cook better when they are a little smaller.

And I can eat a dozen of Mama's Hushpuppies while we are waiting for everything to finish getting ready. Talk about a good appetizer! So plan your fish fry to cover generous servings, lots of standing by the stove and nibbling, and someone eating that last piece of fish on the plate!

Greek Catfish with Garlic White Beans

6 to 8 catfish fillets
1-1/2 tablespoons ground thyme
1/2 teaspoon salt
1/2 teaspoon black pepper
2 tablespoons olive oil
5 tablespoons butter
1 large clove garlic, crushed
2 tablespoons fresh lemon juice
1/2 cup mashed white beans
3 tablespoons minced fresh parsley

Garlic White Beans

16-ounces dried Great Northern Beans
2 quarts salted water
1/2 cup white vinegar
1/2 cup vegetable or olive oil
1 teaspoon garlic powder
1/2 teaspoon salt
2 tablespoons minced parsley

In a large heavy saucepan, cook the dried beans in the salted water over medium heat, until almost done—about 1 hour. They should be tender, but not mushy. Drain. In the same saucepan, toss the beans with the oil and vinegar to coat. Add the salt and garlic powder, continuing to toss the beans. Correct the seasonings to your own taste. (We like a lot of both.) Add the parsley and set aside until needed. The beans can be made 2 days ahead and refrigerated. Warm them up to use with this recipe.

Prepare the Garlic White Beans and keep them warm.

Wash the catfish fillets and sprinkle them with the thyme, salt and pepper. Refrigerate until ready to cook.

When ready to serve, heat the olive oil and 2 tablespoons of the butter in a large heavy skillet. Add the garlic and stir.

Add the catfish fillets and sauté until they are lightly browned, about 5 minutes. Cook in batches if necessary to avoid crowding the fish. Keep fillets warm. Add lemon juice and 1/2 cup of mashed Garlic White Beans to the skillet. Bring mixture to a simmer. Whisk in the remaining butter, 1 tablespoon at a time, then add the parsley.

Serve the catfish fillets on a bed of the White Beans, with the pan juices poured over each serving.

Serves 6 to 8

The Garlic White Beans are fantastic as a cold salad or side dish. So make them hot and fresh for this recipe, and plan on serving any extra beans cold as a salad for another meal.

Ginger-Steamed Catfish with Sesame Sauce

6 catfish fillets
2 teaspoons grated fresh ginger
2 green onions, finely chopped
Toasted sesame seeds to garnish

On top of each catfish fillet, put a bit of ginger and green onion, spreading it along the length of the fish. Place catfish fillets on a plate in a steamer with 2 inches of water.

Bring the water to a slow boil and with the pan tightly covered, steam the fillets for about 15 minutes or until they are white and firm to the touch. Serve immediately with the Sesame Sauce and sprinkle with the sesame seeds.

Serves 6

Sesame Sauce

1/4 cup soy sauce
1/2 teaspoon oriental sesame oil
1/2 teaspoon sugar
2 teaspoons rice vinegar
1 small green onion, finely chopped

Combine all of the ingredients in a small bowl. Stir well to dissolve the sugar. This sauce is rich and should be served in small dipping dishes, or lightly drizzled on top of the steamed fish. Sauce can be made a day ahead.

Makes 1/2 cup

The catfish fillets can be served cold as an appetizer. Cut in bite-size pieces, pile onto a serving dish, sprinkle with toasted sesame seeds, and serve with the dipping sauce. It's a good idea to steam a couple of extra fish for a easy lunch the next day to be served with a salad and a bit of the sauce.

Garlic-Grilled Catfish with Tomato Sauce

4 catfish fillets
6 large cloves garlic, finely minced
1/4 cup olive oil
2 tablespoons white vinegar
1 teaspoon thyme leaves
4 tablespoons chopped parsley, divided
1 tablespoon butter or olive oil
1 cup chopped green bell pepper
1 cup chopped onion
1 cup chopped fresh tomato
1/4 cup red wine
1 green onion, minced for garnish

Wash the catfish fillets and pat dry. Place the garlic, olive oil, vinegar, thyme and 2 tablespoons parsley in a small bowl. Mix well, crushing the garlic against the bowl to release the flavor. Add the dry catfish fillets and coat them well with the mixture. Allow the fish to marinate for at least one hour, overnight is fine.

In a small skillet over medium heat, melt the butter and add the bell pepper, onion and tomato. Simmer for 5 minutes. Add the wine and remaining 2 tablespoons of parsley and simmer for another 5 minutes. This sauce may be made ahead and warmed. When you are ready to serve, preheat the grill and remove the fillets from the marinade. Keep as much of the minced garlic on the fish as possible. Cook the fish fillets over a medium-hot fire for 3 to 4 minutes on each side. Serve immediately, placing the grilled fillet on top of the warm tomato sauce and sprinkle with the minced green onion.

Serves 4

Grilled Catfish—Bouquet Garni

3 teaspoons fennel seed
1-1/2 teaspoons dried tarragon
3 teaspoons dried dill weed
1-1/2 teaspoons white pepper
6 catfish fillets

Place the first four ingredients in a small bowl and blend thoroughly. Keep the mixture in a tightly sealed jar in a dark place and the flavors will remain fresh for several months.

Wash the catfish fillets and pat dry. Place in a glass dish, squeeze the lemon juice over the catfish fillets and sprinkle with the Bouquet Garni mixture on both sides. Refrigerate until ready to cook. The fish can marinate for up to 24 hours while the flavors improve.

When ready to serve, grill the fillets for 4 to 5 minutes on each side. Sprinkle a bit more of the mixture over the fish while it is on the grill, a little falling on the fire will give the fish a nice flavor. Serve immediately with wedges of lemon.

Serves 6

Traditionally the Bouquet Garni was enclosed in a tiny cloth sack and used in poaching or boiling fish or other meats. This wonderful seasoning is excellent, moistened with the lemon juice and sprinkled onto the flesh of the fish. But try the old way too! Put a teaspoon loose into the water or wine you use for poaching fish for a slightly different flavor.

Herb-Grilled Catfish Fillets

6 to 8 catfish fillets
3 to 4 tablespoons fresh lemon juice
2 tablespoons cayenne pepper
2 tablespoons garlic powder
2 teaspoons dried parsley
2 teaspoons ground thyme
2 teaspoons basil
2 teaspoons black pepper
2 teaspoons onion powder
2 teaspoons sage
2 teaspoons marjoram

Wash the catfish fillets and pat dry. Place in a glass dish and sprinkle the lemon juice over the fillets. Set aside.

Place the remaining ingredients in a jar and combine well. The herb mixture may be stored, tightly covered, for several months. Shake the herbs over the fillets, covering both sides of the fish. Allow the fillets to marinate, refrigerated, in the herb and lemon mixture for at least 24 hours.

When ready to serve, grill over a medium-hot fire for 4 to 5 minutes per side, basting with any juices. Serve immediately. Or place under a hot broiler in a pan that will collect the juices, and cook for 3 to 4 minutes without turning the fish. Serve immediately with any accumulated juices.

Serves 6 to 8

Herbs are a marvelous substitute for salt and other less-healthy seasonings. Prepare this herb mixture, keep it handy in a shaker and use it on vegetables at the table or while cooking, and on other grilled meats for flavor without guilt. Of course, a nice dry white wine instead of the lemon juice would be a great marinating partner, but the original recipe is truly healthy, and totally delicious!

Grilled Catfish Fillets Hinote

6 to 8 catfish fillets
1/2 cup melted margarine or butter
Juice of 2 lemons
Lemon-pepper seasoning
Cajun flavored seasoning

Preheat grill for 15 minutes. Mix the melted margarine and lemon juice in a small bowl.

Wash the catfish fillets and pat dry. Place the fillets in a wire fish basket and grill over medium heat. Baste the fillets frequently on each side with the lemon-butter, turning the basket often to prevent burning. Sprinkle lemon pepper seasoning on each side. Total cooking time should be about 10 minutes. Before serving, sprinkle the cajun flavored seasoning on each side.

Serves 6 to 8

Sam Hinote shared this recipe with me when it was printed on a barbecue apron years ago. This is so easy and proves once again that there are more ways to cook catfish than with a frying pan. And Ren's Mint Tea is a must for backyard cookouts. Try it! It's wonderfully refreshing and so Southern.

Ren's Mint Tea

1 gallon water
6 regular tea bags
10 springs fresh mint
6 to 8 lemons (1 cup juice)
2 cups sugar

Squeeze lemons and reserve the rinds. If juice docs not measure 1 cup, add frozen lemon juice. Bring water to a boil. Turn the heat off, leaving the boiler on the stove. Add lemon rinds, tea bags and mint. Let the tea steep for 1 to 2 hours.

Remove the tea bags, mint and lemon rinds. Add the sugar and lemon juice, stirring well. Strain the tea and chill.

Makes 1 gallon

It will be delicious for 2 to 3 days, if it lasts that long. As Ren says, it is "best enjoyed on a screened porch with good friends."

Lemon-Grilled Catfish

1/2 cup Worcestershire sauce
1/3 cup lemon juice
1/2 teaspoon cayenne pepper
4 drops Tabasco
1/2 teaspoon ground thyme
6 to 8 catfish fillets
Lemon wedges for garnish

Mix all the seasoning ingredients in a jar with a tight fitting lid and shake well to mix thoroughly. The marinade will keep in the refrigerator for several weeks, if you do not use it all.

Wash the catfish fillets and pat dry. Cover the fillets with the marinade and refrigerate for at least 1 hour, or up to 4 hours. Grill over a medium-hot fire, basting with the marinade and turning the fish several times. Cooking time will be about 10 minutes. Serve immediately with a wedge of lemon or Apple-Pepper Salsa.

If you do not want to grill the fish, melt a tablespoon of butter in a heavy skillet on high heat. Place the fillets in the hot skillet, shaking it to prevent sticking. Cook the fish, turning once, for 3 to 4 minutes until done. Serve immediately.

Serves 6 to 8

The marinade is wonderful on catfish fillets, fresh shrimp and even on steaks. So double the recipe and you'll have some extra to "stock" your refrigerator.

Apple-Pepper Salsa

1 green or yellow bell pepper, chopped
1 ripe tomato, chopped
1 unpeeled Red Delicious apple, chopped
1/2 cup chopped red onion
1 large jalapeño chili, minced
2 tablespoons olive oil
1 tablespoon lemon juice
1/2 teaspoon salt
2 tablespoons fresh cilantro, if available

Mix all the ingredients in a bowl, blending well.
Refrigerate for several hours before using. The Salsa can be
refrigerated for several days and served with fresh green beans
or as a dip with tortilla chips.

Makes 3 cups

Orange-and-Thyme Grilled Catfish

4 catfish fillets
2 teaspoons grated orange rind
2 tablespoons minced green onion
1 teaspoon salt
2 tablespoons brown sugar
1 teaspoon ground thyme
1/2 teaspoon pepper
3 tablespoons fresh lemon juice

Wash the catfish fillets and pat dry. Set aside on absorbent paper. In a small bowl mix the orange rind, onion, salt, sugar, thyme and pepper, blending thoroughly. Rub both sides of the catfish fillets with the sugar mixture and place fillets in a glass bowl to marinate. Sprinkle the fresh lemon juice over the fillets and turn several times in the bowl to completely coat. Cover tightly and refrigerate. The fish should marinate overnight for best flavor, but a bit longer doesn't hurt.

Grill the catfish fillets over a medium fire until done, 4 to 5 minutes per side depending on the thickness, basting with any remaining juices. Or place under a hot broiler in a pan that will collect the juices, and cook for 3 to 4 minutes without turning the fish. Serve immediately with a simple buttered pasta and marinated fresh vegetables.

Serves 4

This do-ahead recipe will double or triple easily. It is also one of those recipes that allows you to substitute what you have on hand for what is suggested in the directions. We have made this with lemon rind instead of orange rind, white wine instead of lemon juice, even a dry red wine or brandy works beautifully. All the variations are good, we just happen to like the unlikely flavor of the orange rind the very best.

Catfish Madagascar

4 catfish fillets
2 tablespoons green peppercorns
(available at specialty food stores)
2 tablespoons butter
2 tablespoons minced green onions
1/2 cup chicken stock
1 tablespoon tomato paste
1/4 cup brandy
3 tablespoons butter, softened

Wash the catfish fillets and pat dry. Press the green peppercorns onto both sides of each fillet. You want them to adhere to the fish. This can be done several hours before cooking the fish.

In a heavy skillet, melt 2 tablespoons butter, add the green onions and cook for 1 minute. Add the catfish fillets and saute for 2 to 3 minutes on each side. Remove to a plate and keep warm.

Pour the chicken stock into the same skillet. Add the tomato paste. Boil down rapidly, scraping the juices from the bottom and sides of the skillet. Add the brandy and boil for another minute. Remove from heat and stir in the butter, 1 tablespoon at a time.

Serve immediately on plates with the green peppercorn sauce over the catfish fillets. Pass any extra sauce at the table.

Serves 4

A variation of this recipe has been a staple of our kitchen for 24 years. While living in England, we frequented a restaurant outside Cambridge, The De la Poste. The owner did a beef steak with green peppercorns that was absolutely heaven—and we have done a version of our own ever since. This is truly Tony's specialty! He was sure it would be just as good with catfish—and he was right! The sauce is a touch lighter than it is with beef, but you still have to chase down every drop of it on your plate, it is so good!

Marinated Mississippi Catfish

1/4 cup vinegar
1/2 cup vegetable oil
1/2 teaspoon garlic powder
1 teaspoon dry mustard
1/2 teaspoon coarse ground black pepper
1/2 teaspoon salt
1 tablespoon chopped chives
1/2 teaspoon dried tarragon leaves
6 catfish fillets

Thoroughly mix the vinegar, oil, garlic, mustard, pepper, salt, chives and tarragon. Wash the catfish fillets and pat dry. Cover the fillets with the marinade and refrigerate for 24 to 48 hours. Using a fish basket, grill over a medium-hot fire for about 10 minutes, turning the fish and basting with the sauce. Or broil for about 5 to 6 minutes. Use a perforated grill pan that has been rubbed with the marinade before positioning the fish. Do not turn the fish over during the cooking, but do baste with the marinade. Serve immediately.

Serves 6

Fish marinated and cooked like this is scrumptious cold as well! And what a great way to eliminate cooking every night! Serve the fish cold on the second day with one of the great salads in this book, but use this style fish instead of the one suggested in the directions.

Catfish Modena from CICERO's

6 catfish fillets
All-purpose flour
Seasoned salt
1/4 cup olive oil
1/2 cup melted butter
Balsamic vinegar
2 tomatoes, diced
1 tablespoon capers
2 tablespoons chopped fresh parsley
Toasted croutons (optional)

Wash the catfish fillets and pat dry. Sprinkle the fish with seasoned salt. Dredge in flour. In a large skillet, pan-fry the fillets in the oil and butter mixture over medium heat. Cook the fish until they are golden brown. Drain on absorbent paper.

Place the cooked fillet on each serving plate and dash the cooked fish with Balsamic vinegar. Garnish the fish with the diced tomatoes, capers, parsley and croutons.
Serve immediately.

Serves 6

Jimmy and Becky Walker opened CICERO's Restaurant in 1984 in Stoneville, Mississippi. They originally planned to serve only sandwiches and barbecue but it wasn't long before other items were added to the menu. Now they offer many menu selections. Catfish is one of their specialties, serving 6 catfish dishes every night: Blackened, Broiled, Stuffed, Fried, the Modena described here, and Catfish CICERO, which is also included in this book. Our thanks to the Walkers for sharing with us and for promoting catfish at CICERO's, the 1992 Mississippi Magazine's *Reader's Choice Award winner!*

Moussaka
(Eggplant and Catfish Casserole)

1 large eggplant, sliced 1/4-inch thick
6 catfish fillets
1 large onion, sliced
2 cloves crushed garlic
1 tablespoon olive oil
16-ounce can chopped tomatoes, drained
1/2 cup dry white wine
2 tablespoons chopped parsley
1 teaspoon sugar
1/4 teaspoon cinnamon
Salt and pepper to taste

Cream Sauce I

3 tablespoons butter
4 tablespoons flour
2 cups milk
1/4 teaspoon cinnamon
1 teaspoon dry mustard
1/2 teaspoon salt
1/2 teaspoon black pepper
3 tablespoons grated Parmesan cheese
1 egg, slightly beaten

Place sliced eggplant on an oiled baking sheet and broil until lightly browned on each side. Set aside. Sauté the onion and garlic slowly in the hot oil for about 8 minutes. Add the catfish, washed and cut into 1-inch pieces, and continue to cook for 3 minutes, stirring. Add the tomatoes, wine, parsley, sugar, cinnamon, salt and pepper. Simmer for 10 minutes.

To make the Cream Sauce, melt the butter in a heavy saucepan, stir in the flour and cook slowly for 2 minutes. Add the milk, stirring constantly until thickened. Let the sauce bubble for 1 minute. Remove from heat and add the cinnamon, mustard, 1 tablespoon of the cheese, salt and pepper to taste. Just before using, stir in the beaten egg, mixing well.

To finish assembling the Moussaka, butter a 9- by 13-inch baking dish, and place a layer of eggplant in it. Top the eggplant with 1/2 of the fish mixture. Add another layer of eggplant, then the remainder of the fish mixture. Finish with eggplant, if there is more. Spread the Cream Sauce on top and sprinkle with the rest of the Parmesan cheese.

Bake in a preheated 350° oven for about 40 minutes. The top of the casserole should be puffed and golden. The Moussaka can be served immediately or set aside to be reheated later.

Serves 6 to 8

This Moussaka is a wonderful variation of the meaty Greek version. The blend of flavors with less oil, give a truly traditional dish a healthy, delicious new lease on life. And it is a fabulous dish to make ahead. It just gets better with 2 to 3 days in the refrigerator! Served with a green salad (Greek style would be nice) and soft, hot pita bread, it's a complete meal.

Oriental Broiled Catfish

6 to 8 catfish fillets
1 small onion, finely minced
4 tablespoons grated fresh ginger
3 tablespoons vegetable oil
4 green onions, finely chopped
1/3 cup soy sauce
2 tablespoons dry sherry
1 teaspoon sesame oil
1 tablespoon sugar
1/4 teaspoon white pepper
1 green onion, minced for garnish

Sauté the ginger, onion and oil in a heavy saucepan over low heat for 6 to 8 minutes. Pour the remaining ingredients into a glass bowl. Add the onion mixture and stir well.

Wash the catfish fillets and pat dry. Place fish into the marinade and coat well. Allow the fish to marinate overnight for maximum flavor, turning occasionally.

Place the marinated fillets in a 9- by 13- baking dish and spoon the marinade over them. Broil for about 6 to 8 minutes, without turning the fillets. Serve with the pan juices spooned over each fillet. Garnish with minced green onion.

Serves 6 to 8

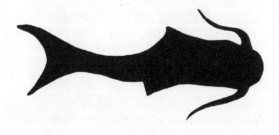

A nest of sautéed fresh spinach is a perfect complement to this subtly flavored dish. Add a serving of buttered linguini and the pan juices for a colorful and delicious light meal.

Pan-fried Catfish with Cilantro Sauce

6 catfish fillets
1/2 cup buttermilk
2 tablespoons butter
1 tablespoon oil
1/2 cup yellow cornmeal
2 teaspoons ground cumin
1/4 cup flour
2 tablespoons grated lemon peel
1/2 teaspoon cayenne pepper

In a shallow dish, combine the cornmeal, cumin, flour, lemon peel and pepper to make the breading mixture. Pour the buttermilk into another shallow dish. Dip 1 fillet at a time into the buttermilk to coat on both sides. Then dip into the breading mixture to coat thoroughly. The dish may be prepared to this point and refrigerated for 2 to 3 hours.

Melt the butter and oil in a heavy skillet over medium heat. Add the breaded fish and cook about five minutes until browned and crusty, turning once. Serve immediately with the Cilantro Sauce and a wedge of lemon.

Serves 6

Cilantro Sauce

2 tablespoons minced fresh cilantro
1/2 cup sour cream
1/4 teaspoon pepper
1/4 teaspoon salt
2 tablespoons fresh lemon juice

Mix all ingredients in a glass bowl and set aside. The sauce can be made 24 hours in advance and will improve in flavor.

Makes 1/2 cup sauce

You'll find lots of ways to serve the Cilantro Sauce. It even makes a good dip for fresh vegetables—and it's wonderful with the Catfish Saté.

Catfish en Papillote

6 catfish fillets
1 cup water
1 cup dry white wine
1 bay leaf
3 slices lemon
4 tablespoons butter
Salt and pepper to taste
6 fresh mushrooms, thinly sliced
12 spears fresh asparagus
2 green onions, minced
1 carrot, julienned
1 sprig of fresh fennel
Parchment paper

Wash the catfish fillets and pat dry.

In a large saucepan, mix the water, wine, lemon slices and bay leaf. Bring the liquid to a gentle simmer. Put the catfish into the simmering broth and gently poach the fillets for 6 to 8 minutes or until just cooked. Remove the fillets and set aside to drain.

Bring the poaching liquid to a rolling boil and reduce the liquid to 1/2 cup. Add the butter in pieces and mix it in well. Taste the broth and add salt and pepper to taste. Set aside.

Have all your vegetables sliced before you begin to assemble the parchment packages. Do not assemble more than 3 hours before you plan to serve. You do not want to risk the packages becoming soggy with the butter sauce. Cut pieces of parchment into squares the width of the paper. Lightly fold in half and cut a heart shape of the paper.

Lay each piece of parchment on a flat working surface. Lightly butter the center of the paper, where the fillet will be placed. Center the fillet on the paper. Divide the vegetables among the six fillets, placing them directly on top of the fish. Drizzle the butter sauce over the vegetables and top with a pinch of the fresh, feathery fennel leaves.

Close the parchment by folding and creasing the edges of

the paper tightly, pulling the paper up so that no
juices can escape. Place parcels on a lightly buttered baking sheet, but do not crowd. The parcels
can wait, refrigerated, for up to 3 hours before baking.

When you are ready to serve, place the parcels in a preheated 400° oven for 7 to 8 minutes. This will be enough time
for the fish to heat, the vegetables to steam, and the parchment to puff and brown lightly. Serve immediately.

Serves 6

*A really elegant presentation! The fish is delicately flavored
and the steamed vegetables are perfect! The parcel will fill most
plates so a simple side dish is adequate— maybe fresh asparagus
with a vinaigrette dressing and roasted red and yellow peppers, or
this wonderful Spinach Salad, plain or topped with chopped
artichoke hearts and mandarin oranges. And such an easy dish to
serve guests! Everything done before they arrive and only 10
minutes in the kitchen to finish dinner! Enjoy!*

The Crown's Spinach Salad

1/2 cup onion, chunked
1/3 cup white vinegar
1/3 cup ketchup
2 tablespoons Worcestershire sauce
1/2 teaspoon salt
3/4 cup sugar
1 cup vegetable oil
1 large package fresh spinach

To make the dressing, put the onion, vinegar, ketchup,
Worcestershire sauce and salt in the jar of a blender or food
processor and blend for 1 minute. Slowly sprinkle the sugar
into the blender while it is running, to dissolve the sugar.
Then very slowly, drizzle the oil into the running blender so
that the oil is emulsified completely and the dressing is
smooth. The dressing will hold in a covered container in the
refrigerator for a week.

Just before serving the salad, combine the spinach with a
small amount of the dressing to lightly coat the leaves. You
will have enough dressing for several salads, so enjoy.

Phyllo Wraps with Mushrooms and Catfish

4 catfish fillets
2 tablespoons butter
4 ounces mushrooms, sliced
1/2 cup chopped green onions
2 tablespoons chopped celery leaves
1/2 teaspoon dried tarragon
1/4 teaspoon salt
1 teaspoon ground black pepper
1 cup grated Swiss cheese, divided
1 package phyllo pastry
1/2 cup melted butter

Wash the catfish fillets, pat dry and place on absorbent paper until needed. In a small saucepan, over medium heat, melt 2 tablespoons butter. Add the mushrooms and green onions and cook for 1 to 2 minutes. Do not brown. Take off heat. Add the celery leaves, tarragon, salt and pepper, mixing well. Set aside.

Melt 1/2 cup butter and set aside. Open the phyllo package and lay the pastry on a flat surface. Place one sheet of pastry on the working surface and keep the remainder covered with waxed paper and a slightly damp cloth. Brush the sheet of pastry with butter and place another sheet on top of the first. Continue buttering and stacking the third and fourth sheets of pastry. Butter the top surface of the sheet.

On the short side of the pastry, lay one catfish fillet. On top of the fillet, place 1/4 of the mushroom mixture and 1/4 of the grated cheese. Fold in the sides of the pastry to make an envelope, then roll the pastry enclosing the fillet in the phyllo envelope, sealing any loose edges with butter. Try to position the envelope so that the seam is placed down on the lightly buttered baking sheet and the filling is up. Butter the top and sides of the pastry parcel. The pastry will hold refrigerated at this point for several hours.

When ready to serve, bake in a preheated 400° oven for 20 to 25 minutes or until nicely browned. Serve immediately.

Serves 4

This recipe can be multiplied or cut easily. The pastry parcels look lovely on the plate. And they hold their heat so well, it's even a nice dish to serve for a dinner buffet, when serving takes extra time. A sauce isn't necessary, but Hollandaise is always a good choice if you prefer the look and color of a sauce. This is so simple but looks and tastes much more complicated than it is!

Poached Catfish with Lemon-Dill Sauce

6 catfish fillets
3 cups water
1/2 medium onion, sliced
2 tablespoons fresh lemon juice
1/2 teaspoon coarse ground pepper
1/2 teaspoon salt
2 bay leaves

Put water and all seasonings into a heavy saucepan and bring to a boil. Reduce heat and let the mixture simmer for 15 minutes. Add the catfish fillets to the poaching liquid and bring the liquid back to a gentle simmer. Cook 6 to 8 minutes or until the fish is just cooked through. Carefully remove the fillets from the liquid and drain. Refrigerate until ready to use. Serve the cold fillet on a bed of fresh salad greens topped with the Lemon-Dill Sauce.

Serves 6

Lemon-Dill Sauce

2 teaspoons fresh lemon juice
1 teaspoon grated lemon peel
1 clove garlic, minced and pressed
2 teaspoons dillweed
1 cup mayonnaise
1/4 cup buttermilk (or plain yogurt)

Mix all ingredients in a small glass bowl and refrigerate. This sauce can be made 2 days ahead.

Makes 1-1/2 cups

The poached fillets can be held refrigerated for 2 days, so it is helpful to cook a couple of extra fillets to use for a quick meal later in the week. You can serve the fish warm by heating in the microwave or bring the poaching liquid to a simmer again and place the fillets in the water for just a minute to heat through. Drain and serve warm drizzled with the Lemon-Dill Sauce.

Poisson Provencal

6 catfish fillets
3 cups water
1 lemon, sliced
2 tablespoons butter or olive oil
1 onion, sliced
1 green pepper, thinly sliced
2 cloves garlic, minced
1 16-ounce can sliced tomatoes, with liquid
1 cup thinly sliced fresh zucchini
1/2 teaspoon black pepper
1/4 teaspoon salt
1/4 teaspoon thyme
1 tablespoon chopped parsley
1/2 cup dry red wine

In a large saucepan, bring the water and lemon slices to a simmer. Add the catfish fillets and poach gently for about 8 minutes. Remove fillets and drain well.

Discard water. In same pan, melt the butter over medium heat. Add onion, green pepper and garlic. Cook until soft. Add tomatoes, zucchini, pepper, salt, thyme and parsley. Simmer 5 minutes, stirring gently. Add red wine and simmer for another 5 minutes. The sauce can be held, refrigerated, at this point for several hours.

When you are ready to serve, place cooked catfish fillets in a lightly buttered baking dish in one layer, or in individual serving dishes. Cover fillets with the sauce, heaping it on top. Bake at 350° for 15 minutes or until hot and bubbly.

Serves 6

The Provencal sauce is really versatile. Try simmering fresh peeled shrimp directly in the sauce. Add a bit more red wine if necessary for moisture and the resulting broth is delicious! And this is heart healthy—especially if you use the olive oil. Either way the Catfish or Poisson Provencal is a winner. We developed this dish for a dinner meeting of the Mississippi Heart Association and we've loved serving it.

Catfish Quiche

4 catfish fillets
2 green onions, chopped
3 tablespoons butter
2 tablespoons dry sherry
3 eggs
1 cup milk
1 tablespoon tomato ketchup
1/2 teaspoon salt
1/4 teaspoon white pepper
1/2 cup grated Swiss cheese
9-inch pie shell

Preheat oven to 350°. Bake pie shell for about 10 minutes to partially cook it.

Wash the catfish fillets and chop them into small pieces. In a heavy skillet, sauté the green onions and fish in the butter for 2 to 3 minutes, until the fish is white and flakes. Add the sherry and let the mixture bubble for a minute. Set aside to cool.

Beat the eggs and milk together in a bowl. Add the cooled fish mixture and remaining ingredients, mixing well. Pour into the partially baked pie shell. Bake for 1 hour.

Serves 6 to 8

This is a classic quiche recipe using an unusual ingredient—catfish! But the results are predictably wonderful. The quiche will refrigerate until needed, warm up nicely, and even freeze if necessary (or if there are leftovers).

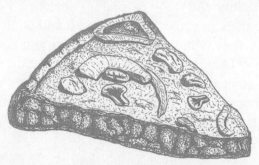

Rice Catalane with Catfish

6 catfish fillets
2 tablespoons vegetable oil
1-1/2 cups sliced onions
1 cup rice, brown or white
1 cup dry white wine
2 cups chicken bouillon
1/2 teaspoon salt
1/2 teaspoon ground black pepper
1 teaspoon garlic powder
1 tablespoon Worcestershire sauce
1 teaspoon ground thyme
Pinch of saffron
2 crumbled bay leaves
2 cups peeled and chopped tomatoes
1 cup grated Parmesan cheese

Wash the fillets and pat dry. Cut the catfish fillets into 1-inch pieces. Place them on absorbent paper and set aside. Heat the oil in a heavy skillet. Add the onions and cook until they are soft. Remove from the skillet into an oven proof casserole and keep warm. In the same skillet, cook the catfish chunks for 1 to 2 minutes. Add the catfish to the onions and keep warm. Add the rice to the same skillet and cook for 2 to 3 minutes, stirring constantly. Scrape the rice into the casserole with the catfish.

Add the wine to the skillet and stir over heat for a minute, scraping all the bits from the bottom of the pan. Pour the juices into the casserole. Add the bouillon, salt, pepper, garlic, Worcestershire, thyme, saffron and bay leaves to the casserole dish. Cover tightly and cook in a 325° oven for 1 hour.

Remove the casserole from the oven and gently stir in the tomatoes. Raise the heat to 375°. Cover and cook for 20 more minutes. The casserole may be made ahead to this point. Reheat carefully to prevent the rice from over-cooking.

Just before serving, carefully fold the cheese into the rice with a fork. Serve immediately.

Serves 6

One of my favorite cookbooks for the past 28 years is Julia Child's Mastering The Art Of French Cooking! *My copy is splattered, flatten-ed, stained, written in, and so well used—it is just embarrassing! But I love it! If I'm uncertain about a dish, I can turn to a section and there is the basic information I need to recreate something wonderful we've tasted or that we THINK might work with the ingredients we have on hand. She even explains what to do in case of disaster!*

So many of the recipes in this book are based on the classic dishes in Mastering The Art Of French Cooking *and Rice Catalane with Catfish is one of those adaptations. I can't begin to thank Julia Child enough for all that her books and shows have meant to us, and for sharing so generously with others her love of cooking.*

Roulades of Catfish

3 tablespoons butter
6 tablespoons all-purpose flour
1-1/4 cups milk
4 large eggs, separated
1 lb SMOKED CATFISH PÂTÉ
(Available at specialty stores or by mail order—see index)
2 SMOKED CATFISH FILLETS
(Available at specialty stores or by mail order—see index)

Line a buttered jelly-roll pan, 15- by 10- by 1-inch, with wax paper. Dust it with flour, tapping out the excess.

In a saucepan, melt the butter and add the flour. Cook the roux over medium heat for 3 minutes, stirring constantly. Slowly add the milk, continuing to stir the mixture for about 5 minutes until thickened.

Transfer the mixture to a large bowl and whisk in the egg yolks, one at a time. Mix well after each addition.

With an electric mixer, beat the egg whites until stiff. Stir 1/3 of the whites into the yolk mixture to soften the batter. Then fold the remaining whites into the batter gently but thoroughly. Spread the batter evenly in the prepared pan. Bake in a preheated oven at 350° for about 25 minutes, or until the cooked sponge is firm to the touch and slightly golden.

Cover the sponge with a sheet of buttered wax paper, buttered side down, and a kitchen towel. Put a baking sheet over the towel and turn the sponge over onto the baking sheet, removing the wax paper carefully from the cooked sponge. Trim 1/4 inch from the short sides of the sponge, so that the roulade will have a trimmed edge when completed.

Let the sponge cool to room temperature, covered with a sheet of wax paper. Remove the paper and spread the sponge with 8 to 12 ounces (or more) of SMOKED CATFISH PÂTÉ, spreading to the edges of the sponge. Mince the SMOKED CATFISH FILLETS and spread the catfish evenly over the pate.

Starting with a long side, roll up the sponge, jelly-roll fashion, keeping the roll as tight as possible without squeezing out the filling. The roulade can be prepared ahead to this point and refrigerated, tightly wrapped, for up to 2 days. Slice diagonally when ready to serve.

Makes about 20 slices

The Roulade of Catfish tastes fabulous—but it looks even more wonderful. It makes a stunning buffet dish! Cut the Roulade in pieces, but leave the roll in one piece on the platter, with bits of the filling showing along the top of the roll, and a few of the end pieces lying flat. Very tempting! Or serve 2 pieces on a plate as a seated first course, or as the "meat" for a salad luncheon. Lovely flavor and texture! You can use the sponge with lots of other fillings as well. Try it with a spinach spread or mushrooms and onions—a mixture of roulades on a plate or platter is a nice way to vary color and flavor.

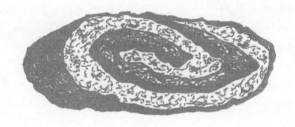

Catfish Royale

6 catfish fillets
3 cups water
1 bay leaf
1 lemon, sliced
1 cup Cream Sauce
1 cup Hollandaise Sauce
1/2 pound crab meat or cooked,
 peeled shrimp

Wash the catfish fillets. Bring the water and seasonings to a slight simmer. Add the fillets and poach very gently, in barely simmering water for 6 to 8 minutes. Remove and drain. The fish may be poached 24 hours ahead and refrigerated until needed.

Mix the Hollandaise Sauce and the Cream sauce with the crab meat, stirring to blend thoroughly. Set aside. Place the catfish fillets on a lightly buttered baking sheet. Divide the sauce mixture between the fillets, covering the fish completely and evenly. You may prepare the dish to this point and refrigerate. When you are ready to serve, run the fish under a hot broiler, for 4 to 5 minutes. This will heat the fish and lightly brown the sauce topping. Serve immediately.

Serves 6

Hollandaise Sauce

3 egg yolks
2 tablespoons fresh lemon juice
1/4 teaspoon salt
Dash of cayenne pepper
1/2 cup butter, melted and bubbling
 when added

In the blender jar, put the yolks, lemon juice, salt and pepper. Let the blender run for a few seconds, then add the hot,

foaming butter in a slow stream. Use the sauce immediately or refrigerate until needed.
Makes about 2 cups

Cream Sauce II

2 tablespoons butter
2 tablespoons flour
1 cup milk
2 tablespoons dry white wine
1 teaspoon dry mustard
1/4 teaspoon garlic powder
Salt to taste

Melt the butter in a heavy saucepan. Add the flour and stir constantly, allowing it to bubble for 1 or 2 minutes. Do not brown. Slowly add the milk, continuing to stir while the sauce thickens. Add the wine and seasonings and stir until smooth. Use immediately or refrigerate until needed.

Makes about 1 cup

The Catfish Royale was first served in 1983, to a group of food editors who toured the Delta's catfish industry, the hatcheries, the ponds and the plants. For lunch, Carolyn Ann Sledge and I served a salad course of SMOKED CATFISH with marinated vegetables and Catfish Royale as the main dish.

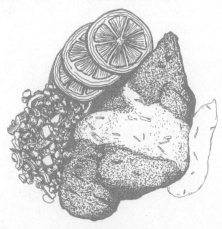

Ranch-Style Baked Catfish Fillets

4 to 6 catfish fillets
1 small bottle Original Ranch Dressing
1 cup grated cheddar cheese
1 cup crushed potato chips

Wash the catfish fillets and pat dry. Place in a shallow, lightly buttered baking dish. Pour the Ranch Dressing over the fillets. Cover with the cheese and top with the potato chips. Bake at 350° for 30 minutes. Serve immediately.

Serves 4 to 6

Could anything be easier? And the taste is great! Two of Indianola's really good cooks — Seymour Johnson and Leet Maggio— suggested this to us. We all need this sort of ultra-reliable, quickly prepared meal for hectic days. Serve the baked catfish with spinach linguine and a medley of stir-fried fresh vegetables piled on slices of ripe tomatoes. Nutritious and delicious! Or serve it with this wonderful Corn and Bean Salad. The salad looks like it makes enough for a small army, but it tastes so good, it will disappear in no time.

Corn and Bean Salad

1 16-ounce can green lima beans
1 16-ounce can small English peas
1 16-ounce can garbanzo beans
1 16-ounce can kidney beans
1 16-ounce can pinto beans
2 16-ounce cans whole kernel corn
1 can sliced water chestnuts
16-ounce jar sweet pickle relish
1 teaspoon garlic powder
1/2 cup sugar
1 cup mayonnaise
1 large onion, chopped
Salt and pepper to taste

Drain and rinse all the canned vegetables. Stir in all other ingredients. Cover and refrigerate for at least 12 hours. This will keep for 7 to 10 days in the refrigerator, if it lasts that long!

Serves 10 to 12

Sassy-Seasoned Catfish Strips

2 cups salt
1-1/2 ounces black pepper
2 ounces cayenne pepper
1 ounce garlic powder
1 ounce chili powder
1 ounce paprika
6 catfish fillets
1 to 3 tablespoons butter

For the Sassy Seasoning mixture, combine the first six ingredients in a glass jar with a tight fitting lid. This mixture will keep forever!

Wash the catfish fillets. Cut the catfish fillets into nuggets or strips. You should get 5 to 6 pieces from each fillet. Lightly sprinkle the fillets with the seasoning mixture. It is salty and it is HOT so you will need to adjust the amount you use to your own taste.

In a heavy skillet, melt a tablespoon of butter. When it is hot, add a few of the seasoned catfish strips. Shake the skillet and nudge the fish with a spatula to prevent the pieces sticking. You want them to be lightly browned and cooked through, but with the heat high enough to seal the juices in. Remove the cooked pieces and add more butter as needed to finish the rest of the strips. Serve immediately.

Serves 6

These catfish nuggets are a great pick up food! And be sure to try the seasoning with strips of chicken breasts. They are so easy to pick up and are good on their own or dipped in almost any sauce. The strips hold their heat well on the buffet table, and even stone cold they are still delicious!

I also like to serve the catfish strips with a buttered pasta and freshly steamed vegetables. I know this mixture sounds salty and it can be if you use too much of the seasoning. But the flavor is terrific! And if you use a non-stick pan instead of butter, the dish becomes low fat and so tasty!

Sautéed Catfish Fillets with Pecan-Basil Sauce

1 cup fresh basil
1 cup fresh parsley
1/2 cup olive oil
1/2 cup chopped pecans
2 cloves garlic, minced
1/2 cup grated Parmesan cheese
1/2 cup grated Romano cheese
2 tablespoons butter, in pieces
6 catfish fillets
1-1/2 cups flour
1 tablespoon cayenne pepper
2 teaspoons salt
2 tablespoons vegetable oil
2 tablespoons butter
Toasted pecan halves, to garnish

Chop the basil and parsley in a food processor. Add the olive oil, pecans, garlic, cheeses and butter. Process into a paste or thick sauce. Add salt to the sauce as needed and set it aside. The sauce can be refrigerated for several days or frozen until needed.

When ready to serve, put the flour, cayenne pepper and salt in a large bowl and mix well. Wash the catfish fillets, coat with the flour mixture and set them aside while the oil and butter heat in a large skillet. When the butter is foaming, add the fillets and sauté until lightly browned, about 3 to 4 minutes. Turn the fillets over and spread the cooked side with the Basil Sauce. Continue to cook for another 3 to 4 minutes until the fish is done. Add more butter and oil to the pan when needed for the rest of the fillets. Serve immediately, garnished with toasted pecan halves.

Serves 6

Toasted, salted pecans have always been a favorite Southern snack food, traditional parts of holiday nibbling, cocktail buffets adn wedding cake plates. Southern cooks have always used almonds on fish and chicken dishes, but only recently begun to use pecans in these same ways! Pecans, wonderfully flavorful, moist and slightly oily, they will substitute for almonds or walnuts in almost any dish! Now if we could just teach the rest of the country how to pronounce—PECAN!

Sesame-Baked Catfish

2 tablespoons toasted sesame seeds
6 catfish fillets
1/2 teaspoon salt
2 cups soft bread crumbs
1/2 teaspoon black pepper
1/2 teaspoon ground thyme
1/3 cup melted butter
Lemon wedges for garnish

Toast the sesame seeds in a dry skillet over medium heat for 3 to 4 minutes, shaking them frequently. Set aside.

Wash the catfish fillets and pat dry. Sprinkle a touch of salt over each fillet. Set aside.

Melt the butter in a medium saucepan. Add the bread crumbs, sesame seeds, pepper and thyme, mixing well. Place the fillets in a buttered baking dish. Cover the fillets completely with the crumb mixture, pressing the crumbs onto the dried surface of the fish. Bake in a preheated 350° oven for 25 minutes, or until crumbs are browned. Serve immediately with a wedge of lemon.

Serves 6

Whole catfish look great with this crumb coating, and their flavor is wonderful. It might take a few more minutes to cook, but the presentation is very nice. Let them bake "sitting up," curving their tails a bit to help them "sit." A nice vegetable medley would look good nestled in the curve of his body—use THE CROWN's *Zucchini recipe, cutting the squash in strips instead of rounds and add carrot strips. Good color and texture for the plate and palate.*

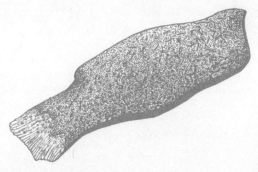

Seafood Crêpes Gratinee

6 catfish fillets
3 cups water
2 tablespoons Old Bay Seasoning
2 tablespoons butter
8 ounces mushrooms, sliced
5 green onions, minced
2 tablespoons chopped parsley
1/2 cup cooked crabmeat
1/2 cup cooked shrimp
2 cups cream sauce
1/4 cup dry sherry (or to taste)
Salt and pepper to taste
16 cooked crêpes
1 cup grated Swiss cheese
Paprika to garnish

Wash the catfish fillets. Cut into bite-size pieces. Place the water and catfish in a saucepan with the Old Bay Seasoning and bring to a boil. Turn the heat off and allow the fish to cool in the water. Drain the fish well. If you are using fresh shrimp, let them cook at the same time in the seasoned water. Peel and drain.

Melt the butter in a saucepan over medium heat. Add the green onions and mushrooms and cook gently for 1 to 2 minutes. Do not brown. Add the seafood, parsley, 3/4 cup of the cream sauce, sherry and seasonings. Mix well. Refrigerate until needed.

Fill the 16 cooked crêpes with the seafood mixture, dividing it equally, and rolling each crêpe into a cylinder. The crêpes may be made ahead to this point, tightly covered, and refrigerated or frozen until ready to serve.

When you are ready to serve, place two crêpes next to each other on a very lightly buttered baking sheet. Warm the cream sauce in a small sauce pan. Cover each pair of crêpes with a bit of the cream sauce, sprinkle with Swiss cheese and run under a hot broiler until the cheese is brown and bubbly and the crêpes are heated through, 3 to 4 minutes. Serve the plates with a bit more of the cream sauce over the crêpes and garnish with paprika.

Serves 8

Seafood Crêpes are wonderful to keep in the freezer for last minute meals! Serve them with a fresh fruit salad, buttered fresh asparagus and hot rolls for an elegant lunch or supper dish.

Our recipe for basic crêpes is so simple. If you have more than you need, the unfilled crépes can be stacked, with a little plastic wrap between each one, and put in the freezer to use later.

Crêpe Batter

3 eggs
1-1/2 cups milk
1 cup flour
2 tablespoons vegetable oil
1/2 teaspoon sugar
1/2 teaspoon salt

In the bowl of an electric mixer, beat the eggs with 1 cup of the milk, the sugar and salt. Add the flour gradually and beat well. Slowly add the remaining 1/2 cup of milk and the oil. Continue to beat for several minutes, until the batter is smooth. If possible, allow the batter to rest for a little while before using. It can be refrigerated for 2 days.

When ready to cook, lightly grease a 8- to 9-inch crêpe pan or heavy skillet. Heat the skillet to a medium high temperature. Pour about 2 tablespoons of batter into the skillet, quickly turning and rolling the skillet to completely cover the bottom. The crêpe will cook fairly quickly. If holes appear in the crêpe, they can be "patched" with a bit more batter. Turn the crêpe over gently with a spatula, to seal and quickly brown the other side. Remove the crêpe and place on a kitchen towel while continuing to cook the remaining crêpes. Cover until needed.

Makes 24 crêpes

Shrimp-Stuffed Catfish

1 small onion, minced
3 green onions, minced
3 tablespoons butter
4 ounces fresh mushrooms, sliced
1/2 cup soft bread crumbs
3 tablespoons chopped parsley
Juice of 1 lemon
1/3 cup butter or margarine
1/3 cup flour
2-2/3 cups milk
2 egg yolks
1/3 cup dry white wine
1/2 teaspoon dry mustard
Dash of cayenne pepper
Salt to taste
6 to 8 catfish fillets
1/2 pound shrimp, cooked and peeled
3/4 cup grated Swiss cheese

For the stuffing: Sauté the onions and mushrooms in butter until tender. Add bread crumbs, parsley and lemon juice, mixing well. The stuffing will hold at this point, refrigerated, for 24 hours.

Make a rich white sauce by melting the butter in a heavy saucepan over low heat. Add flour and cook for 1 minute, stirring until smooth and bubbling. Slowly add the milk, continuing to stir as the sauce thickens. Beat the eggs with a fork. Stir a little of the hot sauce into the eggs to warm them. Add the egg mixture to the sauce, mixing well. Add the wine and seasonings, stirring until the sauce is smooth. Set aside.

Wash the catfish fillets and pat dry. Spread about 2 tablespoons of the stuffing across the center of each fillet and top with the shrimp. Reserve a shrimp to garnish each serving. Roll the fillets and secure with a wooden pick.

Place the catfish rolls, seam-side down, in a lightly buttered baking dish. Spoon a bit of the sauce over each roll. Bake at 350° for 25 minutes. The catfish rolls may be refrigerated at this point for 24 hours and finished in a hot oven just before serving.

When ready to serve, place the catfish rolls in individual baking dishes. Spoon more sauce over the rolls. Sprinkle with Swiss cheese. Bake for 15 minutes to reheat. Place under broiler to melt and brown the cheese. Garnish each serving with a shrimp and a touch of parsley.

Serves 6 to 8

In July 1984, Southern Living *Magazine included THE CROWN in an article about restaurants specializing in catfish. We were thrilled to be a part of this feature on the catfish industry and developed this recipe for their visit and the article. The pictures were lovely, with the toasted cheese and the bubbling sauce. And the taste is just as scrumptious as it looks! This is wonderful to serve house guests—you can do it all before they arrive!*

Southern Sausage with Catfish

2 cups ground catfish (4 to 5 fillets)
1 teaspoon sage
1/2 teaspoon cayenne pepper
1/4 teaspoon coarse ground black pepper
1 teaspoon paprika
1/2 teaspoon sugar
1/2 teaspoon salt
1/4 teaspoon ground oregano
1/4 cup fine fresh bread crumbs

Wash the fillets and cut in 1-inch pieces. Process the fish in the food processor until it is finely ground. Add the remaining ingredients and continue processing until the spices are thoroughly mixed into the fish.

NOW THIS IS IMPORTANT! Test the seasonings by making a tiny patty, a teaspoon full is enough, cook it in a hot skillet, and then taste it! Every section of the country likes their sausage to have a different flavor and you can vary the seasonings to suit your own tastes. Southerners just like to KNOW there is pepper in our sausage! Sage is also an important flavor and we want it to stand up and say that it's there! So test it, change it if you need to, and cook up the rest of those sausage patties!

You can use this Catfish Sausage just as you would any pork sausage—for breakfast, pancake suppers, egg and sausage casseroles—but this is healthier! Use a spray-on fat substitute for cooking, or just a tiny bit of oil to keep it from sticking. You'll be surprised how good it is!

8 to 10 patties

Sour Cream Baked Catfish

8 catfish fillets
8 ounces sour cream
3 ounces Cheddar or Monterey Jack
   cheese, grated
1 can cream of chicken soup
1 tablespoon Worcestershire sauce
1 teaspoon lemon juice
1/2 cup chopped green onions
2 dashes Tabasco

    Wash the catfish fillets and pat dry. Place the remaining ingredients in a small bowl and mix well. Place the catfish fillets in a lightly buttered baking dish. Spread the sauce evenly over the fillets. Cover tightly and bake at 350° for 45 minutes. Serve immediately.

Serves 8

    This is so simple and it is a delicious family or company meal. Serve the fillets on a bed of wild rice with all the extra sauce poured over it. For variety, try rolling the fillet around a 2-inch piece of green onion and placing it seam side down in the baking dish. Bake the rolls just a little longer—it looks a little fancier and tastes wonderful! This will reheat perfectly so "plan" on leftovers!

Soybean Sauté with Catfish

4 catfish fillets
1 cup Lil' Kernel Toasted Soybeans
    or sunflower kernels
1 egg, beaten
2 tablespoons milk or water
1/2 cup flour
2 tablespoons oil or butter, more if needed

Crush the Soybeans or the sunflower kernels in a bag with a rolling pin or in a food processor until they are powdery. Place in a bowl for breading. Put the egg and milk in another bowl and beat lightly to mix. Place the flour in a third bowl.

Wash the catfish fillets and pat dry. Dip each fillet in flour, then in the egg mixture and then in the crushed soybeans. Be careful to coat the fillet completely with the soybeans. Set the fillets aside for a few minutes, if possible, to allow the coating to set.

When you are ready to serve, heat the oil or butter in a heavy skillet over medium heat. Sauté the fillets for 3 minutes or so on each side until cooked through. Serve immediately with a wedge of lemon or Cucumber Sauce.

Serves 4

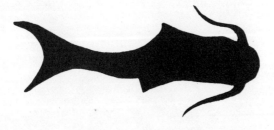

Soybeans are an excellent source of protein and they have no cholesterol! But best of all they have a fabulous flavor and crunch! Soybeans from Mississippi are available in several flavors from specialty food stores or from us by mail order. Sunflower seeds work well too! I just love using two unusual Mississippi farm products in one dish.

Steamed Catfish with Carrots and Asparagus

4 catfish fillets
1 green onion, finely chopped
1 medium carrot, julienned
8 spears of fresh asparagus, julienned
4 tablespoons balsamic vinegar
1 teaspoon dried tarragon
4 teaspoons butter or margarine
4 thin slices of lemon

In individual au gratin dishes or a large baking dish, layer the vegetables to act as a bed for the fish fillets, with the carrots, asparagus and green onion divided equally. Place the fish on top of the vegetables and sprinkle each fillet with 1 tablespoon balsamic vinegar, 1/4 teaspoon dried tarragon and 1 teaspoon butter. Top each with lemon slice. Completely enclose the dish in a sheet of aluminum foil, sealing all edges tightly so that no steam can escape.

Preheat oven to 400° and bake about 8 minutes for indvidual dishes, or 20 minutes for the large pan. Serve immediately.

Serves 4

This dish can be prepared in parchment pouches for an elegant presentation, but I prefer to use the individual dishes. Then all of the wonderful juices created can be captured and enjoyed. Not only is this delicious, but it is really heart healthy.

Spicy Catfish Fingers

6 catfish fillets
1 cup milk
2 tablespoons prepared mustard
2 cups yellow corn meal
1/2 teaspoon salt
1 teaspoon black pepper
1 teaspoon cayenne pepper
1 teaspoon ground oregano
1 teaspoon ground thyme
Peanut oil for frying

Wash the catfish fillets. Cut the fillets in half length wise and then diagonally into 2-inch pieces. Dry on absorbent towels. Whisk the milk gradually into the mustard to make a smooth mixture. Place the catfish pieces into the mixture to soak.

In a large bowl or bag, mix the corn meal with the spices and blend thoroughly. Heat the oil to approximately 375°. Put the catfish fingers into the seasoned meal, a few at a time, and coat thoroughly. Place in the hot oil and cook for just a few minutes until they are nicely browned. Keep them warm in a tightly closed paper bag, until all the fish is cooked. Serve immediately with Coleslaw and Hushpuppies, of course.

Serves 4 to 5

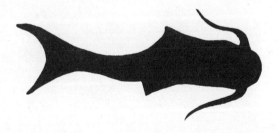

Coleslaw

**1 head of green cabbage, finely
shredded
3 or 4 fresh carrots, grated
1 medium onion, finely chopped
2 green onions, finely chopped
1 cup sweet pickle relish
1/2 cup mayonnaise
Salt and pepper to taste**

Mix all of the above ingredients in a large bowl. Our family likes a bit less of the mayonnaise, but you need to have enough to bind the slaw together. We also use a lot of pepper. Just keep tasting as you season, so you will satisfy your own family's tastes. Try to make the Coleslaw early enough to give it time to sit and blend the flavors. It will refrigerate overnight as well.

Serves 6 to 8

There are tons of variations on good old fried catfish and hushpuppies! It is simply a matter of taste and what your family likes best! But I promise you, they will like it!

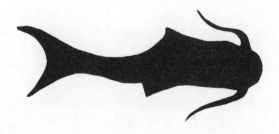

Stir-fried Catfish with Garden Vegetables

3 catfish fillets
3 tablespoons soy sauce
1 teaspoon cornstarch
1 carrot, julienned
1 zucchini, sliced
3 green onions, sliced
1/2 red bell pepper, julienned
6 asparagus spears, cut into pieces
6 mushrooms, sliced
4 large cloves garlic, minced
2 teaspoons minced fresh ginger
2 tablespoons peanut or vegetable oil
2 tablespoons sesame oil
(available in most groceries)

Wash the catfish fillets and cut into 3/4-inch strips across the fillet, and then into 1-inch pieces. Set aside.

Mix soy sauce and cornstarch and set aside.

When all the vegetables are cut and ready, heat the oils in a wok or large skillet. Add the ginger, garlic, carrot and zucchini. Stir for 2 minutes. Add the remaining vegetables and continue to stir for 1 to 2 minutes. Add the fish pieces and stir for about a minute. Add the soy sauce mixture to the wok and continue stirring until the mixture bubbles and thickens slightly, 1 to 2 minutes. Serve immediately over steaming white rice.

Serves 4

Stir-fry dishes are wonderful, quick meals. Everything can be cut ahead of time and wait in the refrigerator until needed. You certainly don't have to have all the ingredients in the recipe above to make a fabulous dinner. Use what you have in the vegetable crisper—delete and substitute! Just be sure that the softer vegetables, like mushrooms, go into the wok toward the end of the cooking time. Try broccoli instead of asparagus! Be creative! Color and variety are important in stir-fry dishes—but the taste at the end is what counts. Remember that a little bit of fish or meat can flavor a huge amount of vegetables.

Sybil's Parmesan Catfish

6 to 8 catfish fillets
1 tablespoon milk
1 egg, beaten
3/4 cup Parmesan cheese
1/4 cup flour
1/4 teaspoon salt
1/2 teaspoon black pepper
1 teaspoon paprika
1/4 cup melted butter
1/4 cup sliced almonds, crushed

Preheat oven to 325°. Combine the milk and egg in a flat dish. Combine the next 5 ingredients in another flat dish. Wash the catfish fillets and pat dry. Dip the fish into the milk mixture and then into the cheese mixture. Place the fillets in one layer in a lightly buttered, flat baking pan. Do not crowd the fish.

The catfish may be held refrigerated at this point for several hours. When ready to serve, drizzle the melted butter over the fillets and top with the almonds. Bake at 325° for about 40 minutes, or until the fillets and almonds are crisp and golden.

Serves 6 to 8

Sybil's Parmesan Catfish is the perfect dish for entertaining a crowd. Put it in the oven and forget about it while you enjoy being with your guests. Isn't that why we have people over in the first place?

The Delta wedding of Sybil and Turner Arant's daughter, Carol, to Larry Brown was the inspiration for several of the recipes in this book. We served catfish fried, smoked and poached—in salads, on cucumbers and our award winning SMOKED CATFISH PÂTÉ for the very first time!

Catfish Thermidor

6 catfish fillets
4 tablespoons butter
1/4 cup finely chopped onion
1 cup sliced fresh mushrooms
5 tablespoons flour
1-1/2 cups milk
1 cup cream
1 teaspoon dry mustard
1 teaspoon celery salt
1-1/2 teaspoons salt
1/4 teaspoon cayenne pepper
2 egg yolks
1 cup grated Swiss cheese
4 tablespoons dry white wine
Juice of 1 lemon

Wash the catfish fillets and cut in 1-inch chunks. Place the milk in a pan, add the fish and poach for 6 to 8 minutes. Lift the fish out and set aside.

In a heavy sauce pan, cook the butter, onion and mushrooms, stirring for 2 minutes. Add the flour and stir until smooth and bubbly. Slowly add the poaching liquid and cream, stirring until thickened and smooth. Stir in the mustard, celery salt, salt and pepper. Add 2 tablespoons of the hot mixture to the egg yolks to warm them. Stir the warmed yolks carefully into the sauce, mixing well. Add the cheese, wine and lemon juice, stirring until smooth. Carefully add the catfish chunks so that they are well mixed but do not completely break apart.

You can hold the Thermidor at this point for several hours, refrigerated. When ready to serve, heat slowly on top of the stove or place in a buttered baking dish in a 350° oven for about 20 minutes. Serve immediately over rice or in pastry shells.

Serves 6 to 8

This has been a family favorite for 26 years! With our cold Green Bean Salad and hot bread, it is outstanding!

Green Bean Salad

1 large can green beans
2 small cans red kidney beans
1 medium onion, sliced
1 medium green pepper, sliced
1-1/2 cups sugar
2 teaspoons salt
1 teaspoon coarse ground black pepper
1 cup salad oil
1-2/3 cups vinegar

Drain and rinse the cans of beans. Place the remaining ingredients in a large bowl, stirring well to thoroughly dissolve the sugar and mix the dressing ingredients. Add the beans and gently stir together. Refrigerate until needed.

The salad can be made 2 to 3 hours before serving, but the flavors really benefit by marinating for 24 hours.

Serves 8

Tortilla, Cheese and Catfish Wrap

4 catfish fillets
1 tablespoon butter
1 large onion, chopped
4 ounces mushrooms, sliced
1 small can green chilies, undrained
4 ounces Monterey Jack cheese, grated
4 ounces sharp Cheddar cheese, grated
4 flour tortillas

Wash the catfish fillets and pat dry. In an oven proof skillet (I use a black iron one), sauté the catfish fillets in the butter until done, about 3 minutes per side. Remove the fillets.

In the same skillet, adding a bit more butter if necessary, sauté the onions and mushrooms for 2 to 3 minutes. Add the green chilies and mix well. Place the fillets back into the skillet, using some of the onion mixture on top of the fish. Mix the cheeses and sprinkle over the skillet, completely covering the fish and onion mixture. Place the skillet under a hot broiler for a few minutes, until the cheeses are completely melted and very lightly browned.

Serve immediately by placing a fillet and accompanying cheese and vegetables on a warm tortilla, folding the edges over to enclose the serving. Place each tortilla on a bed of shredded lettuce and serve with Tomato Salsa and a dollop of guacamole.

Serves 4

This is such an easy entree that becomes a full meal with the shredded lettuce and salsa. (The one skillet clean up is a nice plus as well.) Prepare this recipe as part of a large Mexican meal by leaving out the fish, and serving it as a stuffing for warm, flour tortillas. You can put the hot skillet in a basket right on the table for serving.

Tomato Salsa

2 tomatoes, finely chopped
2 jalapeño peppers, finely chopped
1/2 small onion, finely chopped
3 green onions, finely chopped
2 tablespoons white vinegar
1/2 teaspoon ground cumin
1 teaspoon salt

Combine all ingredients and mix well. Prepare one day ahead, if possible, and store refrigerated.

Makes 2 cups

Tomato Stuffed with Catfish and Feta

4 catfish fillets
2 ripe medium tomatoes, to chop
4 large tomatoes, to stuff
3 tablespoons olive oil
1/2 medium onion, chopped
1/2 cup dry white wine
1 teaspoon oregano
2 tablespoons chopped parsley
1/2 teaspoon salt
1/2 teaspoon black pepper
1 tablespoon ketchup
8 ounces feta cheese, crumbled

Wash catfish fillets and pat dry. Cut into strips and set aside.

Peel medium tomatoes. Seed, juice and chop into small pieces. Cut and core the large tomatoes, reserving the meat to chop and use in the dish. Turn the tomatoes upside down to drain while completing the stuffing.

In a skillet, sauté the onion in the hot oil until tender. Add the catfish strips and cook for 2 minutes, stirring. Add the remaining ingredients, except the cheese, and simmer for 5 minutes, stirring constantly. Reserving a bit of the feta for the top of each tomato, add the cheese to the skillet and stir until well blended. The dish may be prepared to this point and refrigerated for several hours.

When ready to serve, fill the tomatoes with the stuffing. (There may be stuffing left over.) Sprinkle the reserved cheese on top of the tomatoes. Bake at 350° for about 20 minutes to heat through. Finish under the broiler to toast the feta lightly. Serve immediately.

Serves 4

This makes a lovely luncheon dish. Serve with buttered fresh asparagus or broccoli, a nice fruit salad and hot rolls. You can also serve the stuffing in a buttered ramekin for an easy, delicious first course.

Whole Fish Steamed in Leaves

4 to 6 whole catfish, head
  and skin removed
Lettuce leaves (or grape leaves
  soaked in brine) to wrap
4 to 6 whole garlic cloves, crushed
1 bunch green onions, chopped
Salt
4 to 6 tablespoons butter
Freshly ground black pepper
White wine

Wash and dry each catfish. Put a crushed garlic clove, a sprinkling of salt and a few pieces of chopped green onion into the cavity of each fish. Cover each fish with the leaves, completely enclosing the flesh of the fish, with only the tail exposed. The leaves will adhere to the fish naturally. Set aside.

Butter a baking dish that will hold the fish without crowding. Sprinkle the remaining green onions in the baking dish and place the wrapped fish on top. Divide 1 tablespoon of butter along the top of each fish in pats and add the freshly ground pepper. (You can use less butter than this with excellent results.) The fish may be prepared to this point and held, refrigerated, for several hours before baking.

When ready to bake the fish, pour a little white wine over each fish and a bit more into the dish. Bake at 425° for about 20 minutes. (Plan on 10 minutes baking time per 1 inch of thickness of the fish.) Carefully place the wrapped fish on each serving plate. Add a touch of wine to the baking pan to release more of the pan juices and scrape the pan. Divide the juices over each fish. Serve immediately.

Serves 4 to 6

The catfish is absolutely spectacular in this dish—served in solitary splendor on lovely china, with the natural juices poured over it—gorgeous and delicious! You can prepare this for 2 or 20 with great ease following these simple directions.

Serve the fish with a generous side dish of salad and lots of crusty bread. I really like the grape leaves a little better than the lettuce for wrapping, but both are good. Fillets will work with this dish as well, and they will fit into individual serving dishes, capturing all the juices. Cut the cooking time to about 12 minutes for fillets, but use the same technique to prepare. Try this!

Index